Communications
in Computer and Information Science   1674

More information about this series at https://link.springer.com/bookseries/7899

Andreas Ahrens · RangaRao Venkatesha Prasad ·
César Benavente-Peces · Nirwan Ansari (Eds.)

Sensor Networks

9th International Conference, SENSORNETS 2020
Valletta, Malta, February 28–29, 2020
and 10th International Conference, SENSORNETS 2021
Virtual Event, February 9–10, 2021
Revised Selected Papers

 Springer

Editors
Andreas Ahrens
Hochschule Wismar, University
of Technology Business and Design
Wismar, Germany

César Benavente-Peces
Universidad Politécnica de Madrid, Escuela
Técnica Superior de Ingeniería y Sistemas de
Telecomunicación
Madrid, Spain

RangaRao Venkatesha Prasad
Delft University of Technology
Delft, The Netherlands

Nirwan Ansari
New Jersey Institute of Technology
Newark, NJ, USA

ISSN 1865-0929   ISSN 1865-0937 (electronic)
Communications in Computer and Information Science
ISBN 978-3-031-17717-0   ISBN 978-3-031-17718-7 (eBook)
https://doi.org/10.1007/978-3-031-17718-7

This Springer imprint is published by the registered company Springer Nature Switzerland AG
The registered company address is: Gewerbestrasse 11, 6330 Cham, Switzerland

Preface

The present book includes extended and revised versions of a set of selected papers from the 9th International Conference on Sensor Networks (SENSORNETS 2020), held in Valletta, Malta, during February 28–29, 2020, and a set of selected papers from the 10th International Conference on Sensor Networks (SENSORNETS 2021), which was exceptionally held as an online event, due to COVID-19, during February 9–10, 2021.

SENSORNETS 2020 received 35 paper submissions from authors in 20 countries, of which 8.6% were included in this book.

SENSORNETS 2021 received 25 paper submissions from authors in 12 countries, of which 16% were included in this book.

The papers were selected by the event chairs and their selection is based on a number of criteria that include the classifications and comments provided by the Program Committee members, the session chairs' assessment, and also the program chairs' global view of all papers included in the technical program. The authors of selected papers were then invited to submit a revised and extended version of their papers having at least 30% more innovative material.

The use of sensors is familiar to citizens as they are incorporated in many devices including smartphones, vehicles, appliances, and smartwatches, among others. The use of sensor networks is spreading faster everyday, and some examples are their applications in agriculture, health, energy, environment, industry, smart cities, etc. These sensors are usually part of a set of sensors, which are interconnected with each other, and usually with a coordinating (sink) node. Depending on the application and the types of sensors that interact or from which information is collected, the links will be established using different standards depending on requirements: range, bandwidth, power consumption, etc. Due to their configuration flexibility and low cost, wireless sensor networks have been widely deployed. Nevertheless, several issues and challenges must be faced by engineers to guarantee the highest QoS, as security, channel reliability, battery life, interoperability with other networks, etc. Sensor networks performance relies on several impacting factors which must be investigated: network architecture, operating system, hardware implementation, radio interface, protocols, and sensors technology, which must be optimized to achieve the highest availability, reliability, throughput, and power saving. In these networks, each node may be equipped with a variety of sensors, such as acoustic, seismic, infrared, motion, biomedical, and chemical sensors with higher levels of information inference associated with identification, embedded signal processing, and networking of the data.

SENSORNETS intends to be the meeting point where researchers and practitioners share experiences and ideas on innovative developments in any aspect of sensor networks, including sensor networks hardware, wireless communication protocols, sensor networks software, hardware and architectures, wireless information networks, channel characterization, data manipulation, signal processing, localization and object tracking through sensor networks, modeling and simulation, and applications and uses. Papers describing original work were invited in any of the areas listed above. Accepted papers, presented at the conference by one of the authors, were published in the proceedings of SENSORNETS. Acceptance was based on quality, relevance, and originality. There were both oral and poster sessions. Special sessions, dedicated to case studies and commercial presentations, as well as technical tutorials, focusing on technical/scientific topics, were also organized.

The papers selected to be included in this book contribute to the understanding of relevant trends of current research on sensor networks, including embedded systems, the Internet of Things, environment monitoring, smart objects, smart buildings and home monitoring, power management, human-computer interfaces, energy efficiency and energy harvesting, data storage and transmission, and data collection.

We would like to thank all the authors for their contributions and also the reviewers who have helped in ensuring the quality of this publication.

February 2021

Andreas Ahrens
RangaRao Venkatesha Prasad
César Benavente-Peces
Nirwan Ansari

Organization

Conference Co-chairs

Served in 2021

Nirwan Ansari   New Jersey Institute of Technology, USA

Served in 2020 and 2021

César Benavente-Peces   Universidad Politécnica de Madrid, Spain

Program Co-chairs

Served in 2020

Nirwan Ansari	New Jersey Institute of Technology, USA
Andreas Ahrens	Hochschule Wismar, University of Applied Sciences, Technology, Business and Design, Germany

Served in 2021

RangaRao Venkatesha Prasad   Delft University of Technology, The Netherlands

Program Committee

Served in 2020

Agostino Iadicicco	University of Naples "Parthenope", Italy
Ahmad Lotfi	Nottingham Trent University, UK
Ali Emrouznejad	Aston University, UK
Andrea Vitaletti	Sapienza University of Rome, Italy
Antonio Lopez-Martin	Universidad Pública de Navarra, Spain
Anuj Sharma	National Institute of Technology Delhi, India
Boris Kovalerchuk	Central Washington University, USA
Carmen Horrillo	Instituto de Tecnologías Físicas y de la Información (ITEFI), Spain
Chao Tan	Tianjin University, China
Claude Frasson	University of Montreal, Canada
Efthyvoulos Kyriacou	Cyprus University of Technology, Cyprus

Erwin Pesch	University of Siegen, Germany
Fernando Solano	Warsaw University of Technology, Poland
Hui Wu	University of New South Wales, Australia
Lúcio Angnes	University of Sao Paulo, Brazil
Prem Jayaraman	Swinburne University of Technology, Australia
Qiang Wu	Northumbria University, UK
Sergio Trilles	Universitat Jaume I, Spain
Susan Rea	Cork Institute of Technology, Ireland
Ty Znati	University of Pittsburgh, USA
Victor Cionca	NIMBUS Centre for Embedded Systems Research, Ireland
Violet Syrotiuk	Arizona State University, USA
Wei Zhou	ESCP Europe, France

Served in 2021

Achour Mostefaoui	Université de Nantes, France
Eirini Eleni Tsiropoulou	University of New Mexico, USA
Jie Wu	Temple University, USA
José Luis Verdegay	University of Granada, Spain
Niina Halonen	University of Oulu, Finland
Xiang Sun	University of New Mexico, USA

Served in 2020 and 2021

Alberto Ferrante	Università della Svizzera Italiana, Switzerland
Ana Azevedo	Politécnico do Porto, Portugal
Andrzej Szczurek	Wroclaw University of Technology, Poland
Anita Lloyd Spetz	Linköpings universitet, Sweden
Arve Opheim	Sunnaas Rehabilitation Hospital, Norway
Beatriz Lopez	Universitat de Girona, Spain
Benny Lo	Imperial College London, UK
Carlos Marques	Universidade de Aveiro, Portugal
Chia Chong	Sunway University, Malaysia
Christos Douligeris	University of Piraeus, Greece
Dat Tran	University of Canberra, Australia
Dirk Pesch	University College Cork, Ireland
Emmanuel Nataf	Université de Lorraine, France
Fang-Jing Wu	TU Dortmund, Germany
Gabor Paller	Széchenyi István University, Hungary
Gintautas Dzemyda	Vilnius University, Lithuania
Goce Trajcevski	Northwestern University, USA
Ioanis Nikolaidis	University of Alberta, Canada

István Bársony	Institute for Technical Physics and Materials Science, MTA EK MFA, Hungary
Jacek Wytrebowicz	Warsaw University of Technology, Poland
Jadwiga Indulska	University of Queensland, Australia
Klaus Volbert	OTH Regensburg, Germany
Mario Alves	Politécnico do Porto, Portugal
Meng-Shiuan Pan	National Taipei University of Technology, Taiwan, China
Monika Maciejewska	Wroclaw University of Science and Technology, Poland
Orazio Tomarchio	University of Catania, Italy
Prosanta Gope	University of Sheffield, UK
Qammer H. Abbasi	University of Glasgow, UK
Sain Saginbekov	Nazarbayev University, Kazakhstan
Sergey Y. Yurish	IFSA Publishing, S.L., Spain
Sevil Sen	Hacettepe University, Turkey
Stefan Fischer	University of Luebeck, Germany
Weng-Fai Wong	National University of Singapore, Singapore
Xuemin Chen	Texas Southern University, USA
You Li	University of Calgary, Canada
Zhenghao Zhang	Florida State University, USA

Additional Reviewers

Served in 2020

Immo Traupe	University of Lübeck, Germany

Served in 2021

Bennet Gerlach	University of Lübeck, Germany
Jiahui Wen	National University of Defense Technology, China

Served in 2020 and 2021

Florian Lau	Universität zu Lübeck, Germany

Invited Speakers

2020

Steffen Lochmann   Hochschule Wismar, University of Applied
                          Sciences, Technology, Business and Design,
                          Germany
Andrzej Szczurek   Wroclaw University of Technology, Poland

2021

Symeon Papavassiliou   National Technical University of Athens, Greece
Fabrizio Granelli   Università degli Studi di Trento, Italy

Contents

Anomaly Detection in Beehives: An Algorithm Comparison

Padraig Davidson[✉], Michael Steininger, Florian Lautenschlager, Anna Krause, and Andreas Hotho

Institute of Computer Science, Chair of Computer Science X, University of Würzburg, Am Hubland, Würzburg, Germany
{davidson,steininger,lautenschlager,anna.krause, hotho}@informatik.uni-wuerzburg.de

Abstract. Sensor-equipped beehives allow monitoring the living conditions of bees. Machine learning models can use the data of such hives to learn behavioral patterns and find anomalous events. One type of event that is of particular interest to apiarists for economical reasons is bee swarming. Other events of interest are behavioral anomalies from illness and technical anomalies, e.g. sensor failure. Beekeepers can be supported by suitable machine learning models which can detect these events.

In this paper we compare multiple machine learning models for anomaly detection and evaluate them for their applicability in the context of beehives. Namely we employed Deep Recurrent Autoencoder, Elliptic Envelope, Isolation Forest, Local Outlier Factor and One-Class SVM. Through evaluation with real world datasets of different hives and with different sensor setups we find that the autoencoder is the best multi-purpose anomaly detector in comparison.

Keywords: Precision beekeeping · Anomaly detection · Deep learning · Autoencoder · Swarming

1 Introduction

Supporting beekeepers in their care decisions is the goal of precision apiculture. To this end, sensors are used which collect data on 1) apiary-level (i.e. meteorological parameters), 2) colony-level (i.e. beehive temperature), or 3) individual bee-related level (i.e. bee counter) [24]. For colony-level data, environmental sensors are installed in bee hives in order to monitor and quantify the beehive's state continuously. Sensor values we expect most of the times are defined as normal regions of observations, while values differing considerably from this norm are called anomalies. Defining norm and anomaly is always contingent on the context of the analysis. We differentiate between behavioral anomalies, sensor anomalies and external interference. The first anomaly type is characterized by irregular behavior of the bees, the second type occurs when there are irregular measurements due to the sensors, and the last type represents anomalies induced by any external force.

An important behavioral anomaly for beekeepers is swarming, which describes a queen leaving her hive accompanied by worker bees in order to establish a new colony.

© Springer Nature Switzerland AG 2022
A. Ahrens et al. (Eds.): SENSORNETS 2020/2021, CCIS 1674, pp. 1–20, 2022.
https://doi.org/10.1007/978-3-031-17718-7_1

First, there is the *prime swarm* where the current queen leaves the hive with a large number of worker bees. This can be followed by multiple *after swarms* with fewer workers departing. These events can even lead to the complete depletion of a colony [23]. Beekeepers want to prevent swarming as it reduces honey production. Additionally, swarming requires immediate action to recollect the new colonies. Due to the highly stochastic nature of this reproduction process the prediction of these events is difficult.

Anomalies which are not directly related to bees can also occur. On the one hand, there are sensor anomalies which are caused by defective sensors. These require repair in order to restore a beehive's complete functionality. On the other hand, there can be anomalies due to external interference. This usually occurs through physical interaction of the beekeeper with the hive, e.g. when the hive is opened to yield honey.

For large datasets of beehive data it is infeasible to find anomalies manually. Therefore, we apply automatic anomaly detection methods. A number of machine learning algorithms have shown to provide this functionality in other domains. It is therefore interesting to assess how these methods perform in the context of beekeeping.

In this work, we evaluate multiple common anomaly detection models, namely Deep Recurrent Autoencoders, Elliptic Envelope, Isolation Forests, Local Outlier Factor and One-Class SVMs, for their applicability with beehive data. We evaluate these models on three datasets for this work: Two short term datasets, one from [25] and the other from we4bee (https://we4bee.org/), and one long term dataset from the HOBOS (https://hobos.de/) project containing four years of data. These datasets contain labelled swarming events (e.g. observed events by the apiarist) and other anomalies without labels (e.g. hidden or unobserved). The models are trained to find anomalies based on temperature readings of a beehive in an univariate setting (with one temperature sensor) and in a multivariate setting (with three temperature sensors). We use the labelled swarms to assess anomaly detection performance of our models quantitatively. Our results suggest that recurrent autoencoders provide consistently good results across the datasets for both, the univariate and the multivariate setting, compared to the other models. Elliptic Envelope's performance is inconsistent, since it showed by far the best performance when trained on one beehive but also the worst when trained on another beehive. This implies, prediction quality is strongly dependent on the training data. The other models have also shown to provide relatively good performance. Furthermore, we present other types of anomalies found through automatic anomaly detection, namely through the recurrent autoencoder, for which no labels exist and discuss the usage of anomaly detection for non-swarming anomalies.

Our contribution is twofold: First, we compare typical anomaly detection machine learning models for swarm detection in both a univariate and a multivariate sensor setting. Second, we present other types of anomalies found by the recurrent autoencoder in the beehive datasets and discuss anomaly detection for these anomalies.

In this work we present an extension of our work in [6]. This includes a broader spectrum of anomaly detectors, not solely the recurrent autoencoder. Furthermore we added a quantitative analysis of the swarm prediction quality of all detectors. The analysis was done in a univariate sensor setting, as well as a multivariate setting.

This work is structured as follows: Related research is presented in Sect. 2. Section 3 describes the datasets used in this work. The different anomaly detection models of our comparison are presented in Sect. 4. A description of our experiments can be found in Sect. 5 while their results are shown in Sect. 6. We discuss our results in Sect. 7 before concluding the work in Sect. 8.

2 Related Work

There are a number of works which encompass monitoring and detection of swarms in beehives.

Ferrari et al. [8] analyzed humidity, temperature and sound in beehives to understand how these variables change before and during swarming. To this end, they used data from three beehives where nine swarming events had occurred. The authors identified that a change in temperature and a shift in sound frequency might be useful indicators for swarming.

Kridi et al. [11] determined pre-swarming behavior through clustering temperature data. If measurements cannot be assigned to clusters of typical beehive temperature patterns for several hours, the authors consider this an anomaly.

Zacepins et al. [25] proposed an rule-based algorithm for swarming detection using data from a single temperature sensor. Their algorithm (from here on denoted as RBA) detects a swarming event if the temperature is above 35.5 °C for between two and twenty minutes. Events with shorter or longer temperature anomalies are not considered to be swarms.

Zhu et al. [27] link a linear rise in temperature to pre-swarming behavior. They recommend placing a temperature sensor between the bottom of the first frame and the beehive's wall, as this is the most suited location for measuring this increase in temperature.

While some of these works propose swarm detection methods, none of them evaluated a larger set of common machine learning approaches for anomaly detection. Popular models include One-Class SVMs [21], Local Outlier Factor (LOF) [3], Elliptic Envelope [19], Isolation Forests [13] and neural networks [20]. As for neural networks, recurrent autoencoders performed particularly well on sequential data across many anomaly detection settings [4,9,15,22]. Therefore, we evaluate these algorithms to identify which is the most promising for this task.

3 Datasets

We obtained datasets from three sources for our studies: HOBOS, we4bee, and a subset of Zacepins et al. [25] dataset. We selected two HOBOS beehives in Würzburg and Bad Schwartau and one we4bee hive in Markt Indersdorf for our experiments. Zacepins et al. data was collected in Jelgava. From here on, we refer to all datasets by the location of the beehive.

3.1 Würzburg and Bad Schwartau

HOBOS collected evironmental data from five sensor equipped beehives (species *apis mellifera*; beehive type: zander beehive) in Bournemouth, Münchsmünster, Gut Dietlhofen, Bad Schwartau and Würzburg. We selected the hives in Bad Schwartau as there are three verified swarming events. In contrast, data for the Würzburg beehive is completely unverified. We use this beehive to assess cross-beehive applicability of our models. HOBOS beehives come with different sensor configurations. Figure 1 shows the maximum sensor configuration: 13 temperature sensors, named T_1 to T_{11} mounted between the honeycombs and T_{12} and T_{13} mounted on the back and front of the hive respectively, plus weight, humidity, and carbon dioxide (CO_2) sensors. The beehives in Bad Schwartau and Würzburg are both missing some of the temperature sensors: Bad Schwartau is not equipped with T_2, T_3, T_9, T_{10} and T_{12} and Würzburg is not equipped with T_2 and T_3. HOBOS collected data from May 2016 to September 2019. During this time, sensor readings were collected once per minute for every sensor. As the typical swarming period for honey bees is May to September [7], we limit data for our preliminary study to the swarming period. HOBOS granted us access to their complete dataset.

Analysis. The Pearson correlation coefficients between different sensors, e.g. inter-sensor correlations, are visualized in Fig. 8 in the appendix. Within the normal data portion of the dataset, these correlations are strong, especially between adjacent sensors. Correlations are even higher for the sensors T_4–T_{10} placed in the center of the beehive, and go beyond directly adjacent sensors, i.e. sensors T_4 and T_{10} still correlate positively. The sensors placed at the outer margins of the apiary tend to correlate with the sensors placed outside, as well as their opposite counterpart.

During days containing anomalies, correlations are not that strong, except for neighboring sensors. This implies, that certain sensors are more sensible for swarm detection, as also stated in [27].

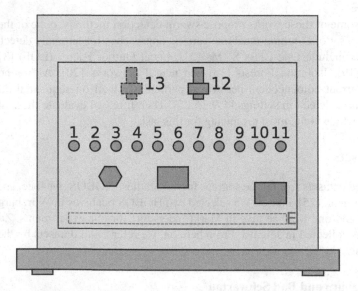

Fig. 1. Back of a HOBOS beehive. Temperature sensors T_1–T_{11} are mounted between honeycombs, temperature sensors T_{12} and T_{13} are mounted on the back and the front of the hive, respectively. E denotes the hive's entrance on the front of the beehive [6].

3.2   Jelgava

Zacepins et al. monitored ten colonies (*apis mellifera mellifera*; norwegian-type hive bodies) with a single temperature sensor placed above the hive. The observation ran from May to August in 2015 and recorded one measurement per minute. The authors recorded nine swarming events during their observation period and granted us access to the nine days in the dataset that contain these events.

3.3   Markt Indersdorf

we4bee started rolling out 100 smart top bar hives to schools and interested individuals all over Germany in 2019. In the same year, first bee colonies have been introduced into the hives. One successful hive of this first project year is the hive in Markt Indersdorf (*apis mellifera*; top bar hive). Figure 2 shows the cutaway view of a we4bee hive: it includes four temperature sensors on the inside of the hive and one on the outside. Three temperature sensors inside the hive distributed along the length of the hive, the fourth is located at the back. The inner temperature sensors are referred to as T_l, T_m, and T_r for the sensors in the hive body; the sensor at the back is named T_i. The outside sensor is called T_o. we4bee hives also report other environmental quantities: air pressure, weight, fine dust, humidity, rain and wind. For Markt Indersdorf we obtained data from June (when the colony was introduced to the hive) to September 2019. All sensors except fine dust reported one measurement per second; fine dust was recorded once every three minutes.

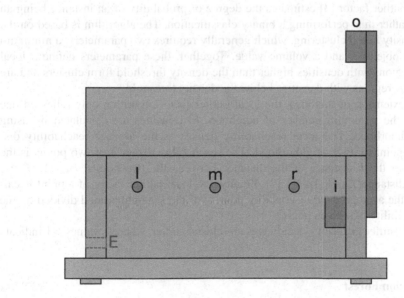

Fig. 2. Cutaway view of a we4bee beehive. T_l, T_m, T_r, and T_i are mounted on the inside, laterally to the honeycombs. T_o is placed outside at the pylon. E denotes the entrance on the front of the beehive [6].

4   Methods

4.1   (Recurrent) Autoencoder

An autoencoder (AE) consists of two neural networks, an encoder ϕ and a decoder ψ. The encoder maps the input space $\mathcal{X}$ into the feature space ($\phi : \mathcal{X} \to \mathcal{F}$). In contrast, the decoder remaps the feature space into the input space ($\psi : \mathcal{F} \to \mathcal{X}$). The task of the encoder-decoder pair is to adapt both mapping steps in a way, that decoding an encoded sequence closely resembles the input itself: $\bar{x} = \psi(\phi(x)) \sim x$. When training the AE with normal data, this kind of data is encoded very well within the feature space, whereas anomalous data cannot be reconstructed properly, incurring a high difference in prediction and input.

This difference is quantified by a loss function $\mathcal{L}$, which is often the l_2 norm [26] or the MSE (mean squared error) [22]. The optimization task can be stated as follows:

$$\phi, \psi = \arg\min_{\phi,\psi} \mathcal{L}(x, \psi(\phi(x))).$$

An anomaly is any input with a resulting loss that is greater than α, which is the anomaly threshold: $\mathcal{L}(x, \bar{x}) \geq \alpha$. This hyperparameter can either be set manually or determined with a labelled anomaly set in a second training step. Optimally, α is set high enough to detect all anomalies, but not too low to be overly sensible within predictions [16].

4.2   Local Outlier Factor

The local outlier factor [3] estimates the degree or probability of an instance being an anomaly, rather than performing a binary classification. The algorithm is based on the idea of density based clustering, which generally requires two parameters: a minimum number of objects k and a volume value. Together, these parameters define a local density. Regions with densities higher than the density threshold form clusters and are separated by regions with densities below the density threshold.

As an extension of this idea, the local outlier factor algorithm only relies on one parameter, the minimum number of neighbors k. Densities are calculated by using the k-heighborhood. The local reachability density is the average reachability distance of a point to its k neighborhood. The reachability distance of two points is the maximum of the k-distance or the distance between the two points: $rd_k(A, B) := \max\{k - \text{distance}(B), d(A, B)\}$ [3]. Finally, the local outlier factor of a point is calculated as the average local reachability density of the k neighborhood divided by the local reachability of a given point.

A local outlier factor of ≤ 1 indicates an (cluster) inlier, whereas values >1 indicate outliers.

4.3   Isolation Forest

While most anomaly detectors build internal profiles of normal data and report anomalies that do not fit in these profiles, the isolation forest is based on the idea of isolating anomalies [13, 14]. An isolation forest consists of several isolation trees, or iTrees. An iTree is a binary search tree, which consists of external nodes (e.g. nodes without children) and internal nodes (e.g. nodes with exactly two children). Internal nodes split the data by a random attribute q and a corresponding split value p. If a data point fullfills the "test" function $q < p$ the path to the first child is followed, otherwise the second path is pursued. This structure is repeated until all data points x in the dataset are isolated in an external node.

Since anomalies are isolated more easily, the path length $h(x)$ for an anomalous point is shorter than for normal data. An anomaly score can be computed as $s(x, m) = \text{pow}(2, -E(h(x))/c(m))$, where $E(h(x))$ is the average $h(x)$ from all iTrees and $c(m)$ represents the average path length given the sample size m. The anomaly score indicates an anomaly if it is close to 1 and normal data for values close to or below 0.5.

4.4 Elliptic Envelope

Elliptic envelope is an anomaly detection algorithm that is based on the minimum covariance determinant (MCD) estimator and assumes the data to be sampled from an elliptically symmetric unimodal distribution. MCD is a highly robust estimator of multivariate location and scatter [18].

The method subsamples the data $\mathbf{X}$ in $\mathbf{H}_1$ and computes an estimate of the location $\mathbf{T}_1$ and the covariance of each sample $\mathbf{S}_1$. A new subsample $\mathbf{H}_2$ is built with the $h = (n + p + 1)/2$ samples with the lowest robust distance [19], where n is the number of samples in $\mathbf{H}_1$ and p the number of features. This subsampling process is repeated until the determinant of the covariance converges within a given tolerance. Elliptic envelope finally flags every sample as outlier that has a robust distance above a cutoff value $\sqrt{\chi^2_{p,0.975}}$ [19].

4.5 One-Class SVM

The one-class support vector machine (SVM) [12], is an extension of the standard support vector machine [5] for unsupervised outlier detection. The SVM algorithm is normally applied to supervised two class classification problems. Input is classified by finding a hyperplane with maximum distance to the closest instances of the two classes. Data points of the same class, in our setting normal data or anomalous data, are grouped on the same side of this plane. To account for datapoints still being non-seperable, a penalty parameter is introduced. The One-Class SVM reuses the SVM algorithm by setting all class labels to the same class. This means, the separating hyperplane is an envelope around the normal data, with a maximum distance towards all anomalies.

5 Experimental Setup

All models described in Sect. 4 are evaluated on the datasets outlined in Sect. 3.

Data Splitting. We used the HOBOS hives for training and validation purposes. That is, we trained on Bad Schwartau and Würzburg in independent settings using the reported and found [6] swarming events. Explicitly, we built two setups: one with training the models on the normal behavior of Bad Schwartau, using its anomalous behavior as a validation set for the parameter search, and one with the training step consisting of the normal behavior of Würzburg, while validating on its anomalous behavior set. The datasets from Jelgava and Markt Indersdorf, as well as the test set from the untrained hive were only used for evaluation. All models were provided with the same splits of input data to ensure comparability.

As customary in novelty detection (i.e. AE, Isolation Forest), the training data shouldn't be polluted by outliers. For that, we visually examined the datastream and marked each day as normal behavior, or as an outlier, e.g. an anomaly. We defined normal behavior as any temperature sensor trace remaining nearly constant at 34.5 °C as the core temperature [8,25]. Any larger deviation form this norm temperature were considered as anomalous days. Figure 3 shows sensor data to be expected from a normal day. Training and validation parts consist exclusively of normal data, while test and holdout sets combine normal and anomalous data. Test sets are any portions of the dataset with anomalous data, that don't originate from the beehive used for training. The holdout set, which contains the anomalous behavior from the training hive, is used for the parameter search of the estimators.

An exemplary view of the data splitting procedure for the Bad Schwartau hive can be seen in Fig. 4. Keep in mind, that the test and holdout sets also contain slices of normal data and are not necessarily only windows with anomalies.

Input Data. In any univariate sensor setting, we use central temperature sensors. For the hives in Würzburg and Bad Schwartau, those are $T_6 - T_8$, from which we evaluate data on T_6 and T_8. In Markt Indersdorf this is T_m, which we additionally downsampled to one minute resolution to be consistent with the other datasets. For Jelgava the single temperature sensor at the top is used. In the multivariate sensor setting, we used senors T_6, T_7, T_8 for the hives Bad Schwartau and Würzburg, whereas we used T_l, T_m, T_r in Markt Indersdorf.

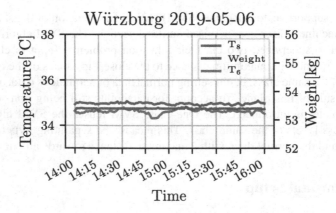

Fig. 3. Normal behavior of all three sensors [6].

Any model is given a 60 min window of sensor data, which corresponds to 60 consecutive input values of temperature data per sensor. According to [8,25,27] swarming events last from 20 min to 60 min in duration.

In the multivariate sensor setting, the AE is provided with sensor data of 60×3, whereas the other models are given $60 \cdot 3$ values, i.e. concatenating the three sensors.

Input data for the AE was normalized via standard scaling (e.g. their z-score). The non-autoencoder models were provided with the raw and unscaled sensor values, since scaling impaired their predictions.

Model Training. The optimal parameter settings for the models were found employing a random search [2]. A table with all parameters that were optimized is given in the appendix (see Table 4). Parameters were optimized using the normal data of a beehive, while using the anomalous behavior of that hive as the validation set for this search. The F_1 score of predicting swarms was used as the metric to be maximized.

For the models Local Outlier Factor, Elliptic Envelope, Isolation Forest and One-Class SVM we relied on the implementations in [17]. In the same setting we searched for the remaining parameter α for the pre-trained AE, which we could not do in [6] due to missing labels. Within this (second) parameter setting step for the swarm detection, we used a windowing technique, shifting the window by 15 min forward in time to extract the next window.

Pre-training of the AE was done in a preliminary random search (see appendix), finding the best hyperparameters for the reconstruction task itself. The *Adam* optimizer [10] was used with the default parameters ($lr = 10^{-3}$) and the mean squared error (MSE) as the loss function. Early stopping with five epoch patience was employed to prevent overfitting. For pre-training, we used all suitable measurement windows by shifting the window one time step further.

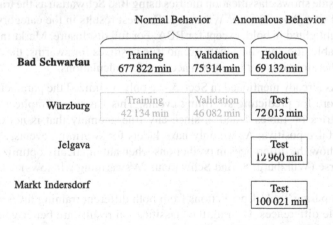

Fig. 4. The data splits used for Bad Schwartau. The autoencoder is trained on Bad Schwartau's 'Training'. The hyperparameters and α are tuned using its 'Validation' and 'Holdout', respectively. The model is then tested on all 'Test'. For Würzburg, the splits are set accordingly using its 'Training', 'Validation', and 'Test' as 'Holdout'. We provide the recording time for all splits [6].

Predictions. RBA [25] is utilized on all anomalous behavior subsets to predict swarming events. We additionally used it on the normal behavior portions of the dataset to ensure no swarming events in the training steps of both training hives.

Predictions with all other models were made by using the best model configuration found in the random search, while predicting events within the tests sets, e.g. the anomalous sets. For instance, a model was trained on Bad Schwartau, using its holdout set for the grid search, while predicting the anomaly sets of Würzburg, Jelgava and Markt Indersdorf.

Evaluation. To evaluate the various classifiers, we used standard classification metrics. *True positives* (TP) contain all time series correctly classified as swarms, whereas *true negatives* (TN) represent all time series correctly labelled as non-swarms. The other two units quantify miss-classifications. *false positives* (FP) are any non-swarms classified as swarms, and *false negative* (FN) any swarms categorized as non-swarms.

With these quantifiers, we can calculate performance measures of the classifiers:

$$P := \frac{TP}{TP + FP} \qquad R := \frac{TP}{TP + FN} \qquad F_1 := \frac{2 \cdot P \cdot R}{P + R}$$

where P represents the precision, R the recall and F_1 the F_1-measure.

6   Results

6.1   Univariate

Table 1 lists the classification metrics for swarming events in the univariate sensor setting for temperature sensor T_8 on the hives Würzburg and Bad Schwartau respectively. The left hand side shows classification metrics using Bad Schwartau as the training hive, the right hand side shows this for Würzburg. The best results in the category precision and F_1 are highlighted in bold, except for RBA. For full disclosure, Markt Indersdorf is listed in this table, too, but since there are no true positives for swarms, the metrics are degrade and therefore it is not taken into account for calculations.

Discussion. As already mentioned in Sect. 5, we only optimized the parameters regarding the F_1 score for predicting swarming events. This has direct implications on the displayed metrics of Tables 1 and 2, since any true anomaly that is not a swarm is reported as a false positive. As we only have labels for swarming events, these tables are meant to show the differences in predictions when automatically optimizing models with very sparse (Würzburg: 8, Bad Schwartau: 24 swarming windows) events and no specialization.

When comparing Table 1 predictions from both different training hives, there are a few remarkable differences: Overall, the classification results are better when training on Bad Schwartau (F_1 : [.09, .12]) in contrast to training on Würzburg (F_1 : [.03, .12]). The main reason for that is the very high inclination of the classifiers towards never predicting a swarming event in Würzburg. Some anomaly detectors even report no true positive for swarming events (Elliptic Envelope, One-Class SVM). Even the metrics on the Jelgava test set decline significantly (Bad Schwartau: F_1 : [.48, .69], Würzburg:

Table 1. Overview of classification metrics and results. Results are only calculated by the true positives of swarms! The estimators are trained on Bad Schwartau on the left hand side and Würzburg on the right hand side (separated by vertical double lines), both with sensor T_8. Precision (P), Recall (R), and F_1 are reported, and set to 0 for no correct classification and F_1 set as NA. Corresponding true positives (TP), false positives (FP), false negatives (FN), and true negatives (TN) values are also reported. The overall metrics are calculated from the weighted scores from each hive.

Classifier	Hive	P[%]	R[%]	F_1[%]	TP	FP	TN	FN	Hive	P[%]	R[%]	F_1[%]	TP	FP	TN	FN
Local Outlier Factor	Jel.	0.32	1.00	0.48	36	78	723	0	Jel.	0.07	1.00	0.13	36	484	317	0
	Wü.	0.01	0.63	0.02	5	485	4268	3	B. S.	0.01	1.00	0.01	24	3925	716	0
	All	0.06	0.68	0.09	41	563	4991	3	All	0.02	1.00	0.03	60	4409	1033	0
	M. I.	0.00	0.00	NA	0	1532	5185	0	M. I.	0.00	0.00	NA	0	303	6414	0
Elliptic Envelope	Jel.	0.5	0.97	0.66	35	35	766	1	Jel.	0.17	1.00	0.29	36	174	627	0
	Wü.	0.00	0.00	NA	0	51	4702	8	B. S.	0.01	0.88	0.01	21	3772	869	3
	All	0.07	0.15	0.10	35	86	5468	9	All	0.03	0.89	0.05	57	3946	1496	3
	M. I.	0.00	0.00	NA	0	58	6659	0	M. I.	0.00	0.00	NA	0	17	6700	0
Isolation Forest	Jel.	0.33	0.75	0.45	27	56	745	9	Jel.	0.21	0.89	0.34	32	121	680	4
	Wü.	0.00	0.50	0.00	4	2443	2310	4	B. S.	0.00	0.50	0.00	4	2443	2310	4
	All	0.05	0.54	0.07	31	2499	3055	13	All	0.03	0.56	0.05	36	2564	2990	8
	M. I.	0.00	0.00	NA	0	5226	1491	0	M. I.	0.00	0.00	NA	0	4056	2661	0
One-Class SVM	Jel.	0.59	0.83	0.69	30	21	780	6	Jel.	0.30	0.89	0.45	32	75	726	4
	Wü.	0.00	0.00	NA	0	298	4455	8	B. S.	0.01	0.88	0.01	21	2255	2386	3
	All	**0.09**	0.12	0.10	30	319	5235	14	All	0.05	0.88	0.08	53	2330	3112	7
	M. I.	0.00	0.00	NA	0	1363	5354	0	M. I.	0.0	0.0	NA	0	204	6513	0
AE	Jel.	0.57	1.0	0.73	37	28	772	0	Jel.	0.50	1.00	0.67	36	36	765	0
	Wü.	0.01	0.50	0.02	4	506	4247	4	B. S.	0.01	0.88	0.02	21	2329	2312	3
	All	**0.09**	0.57	**0.12**	40	535	5019	4	All	**0.08**	0.89	**0.12**	57	2365	3077	3
	M. I.	0.00	0.00	NA	0	251	6466	0	M. I.	0.00	0.00	NA	0	1934	4783	0
RBA	Jel.	1.00	0.50	0.67	18	0	801	18	Jel.	1.00	0.50	0.67	18	0	801	18
	Wü.	0.07	0.25	0.11	2	27	4726	6	B. S.	0.57	0.33	0.42	8	6	4635	16
	All	0.21	0.29	0.19	20	27	5527	24	All	0.64	0.36	0.46	26	6	5436	34
	M. I.	0.00	0.00	NA	0	4	6713	0	M. I.	0.00	0.00	NA	0	4	6713	0

F_1 : [.13, .45]) for all detectors except the AE (Bad Schwartau: F_1 : .73, Würzburg: F_1 : .69).

In both cases, the AE is the best swarm detector within the machine learning algorithms (highlighted in bold). It also seems to be more robust regarding the origin of data, since the F_1 score (0.12) is the same for both training scenarios.

RDA is the best swarm detector regarding the metrics. It does however miss more swarming events (4 vs. 24), some due to the windowing technique used, since in relies on the base temperature 30 min pre-swarming. The major contributing factor for the better metrics performance is the very low false positive rate. This is to be expected, since it is only built for swarm detection and isn't drawn away towards other anomalies and thus inherently has a lower false positive rate. For example, any temperature deviation below 34.5 °C is completely ignored, but may in fact be an anomaly.

6.2 Multivariate

Table 2 lists the classification metrics in the multivariate sensor setting for temperature sensors T_6, T_7, T_8 for the hives Bad Schwartau and Würzburg. Calculation of the metrics is done in the same manner as in the univariate setting. The table lists only the multivariate datasets. The classification metrics of Würzburg are reported when training on Bad Schwartau and vice versa. Furthermore the lines with Markt Indersdorf$_X$ show the reports when training on hive X and predicting Markt Indersdorf.

Table 2. Overview of classification metrics and results in the multivariate setting. Results are only calculated by the true positives of swarms! The estimators are trained on Bad Schwartau predicting Würzburg (and vice versa) and sensor T_6, T_7, T_8. Precision (P), Recall (R), and F_1 are reported, and set to 0 for no correct classification and F_1 set as NA. Corresponding true positives (TP), false positives (FP), false negatives (FN), and true negatives (TN) values are also reported. The overall metrics are calculated from the sum of the number of classifications.

Classifier	Beehive	P[%]	R[%]	F_1[%]	TP	FP	TN	FN
Local Outlier Factor	Würzburg	0	0	NA	0	55	4698	8
	Bad Schwartau	0.005	0.875	0.010	21	4086	222	3
	Overall	**0.005**	0.656	0.010	21	4141	4920	11
	Markt Indersdorf$_W$	0	0	NA	0	5132	1585	0
	Markt Indersdorf$_S$	0	0	NA	0	1055	6552	0
Elliptic Envelope	Würzburg	0	0	NA	0	177	4576	8
	Bad Schwartau	0.006	0.875	0.011	21	4063	578	3
	Overall	**0.005**	0.656	0.010	21	4240	5154	11
	Markt Indersdorf$_W$	0	0	NA	0	3955	3762	0
	Markt Indersdorf$_S$	0	0	NA	0	2842	3875	0
Isolation Forest	Würzburg	0.001	0.500	0.002	4	3206	1547	4
	Bad Schwartau	0.005	0.875	0.011	21	3841	800	3
	Overall	0.004	0.781	0.007	25	7047	2347	7
	Markt Indersdorf$_W$	0	0	NA	0	6694	23	0
	Markt Indersdorf$_S$	0	0	NA	0	6387	330	0
One-Class SVM	Würzburg	0.001	0.500	0.002	4	3206	1547	4
	Bad Schwartau	0.005	0.875	0.011	21	3841	800	3
	Overall	0.004	0.781	0.007	25	7047	2347	7
	Markt Indersdorf$_W$	0	0	NA	0	6694	23	0
	Markt Indersdorf$_S$	0	0	NA	0	6387	330	0
AE	Würzburg	0.001	0.125	0.002	1	1292	3461	7
	Bad Schwartau	0.007	0.875	0.015	21	2841	1800	3
	Overall	**0.005**	0.688	**0.011**	22	4133	5261	10
	Markt Indersdorf$_W$	0	0	NA	0	6683	43	0
	Markt Indersdorf$_S$	0	0	NA	0	5534	1183	0

Discussion. In the multivariate setting, the AE is also the best option for detecting anomalies. Still Table 2 shows, that all metrics drop in contrast to the univariate, single temperature sensor setting. The reason for that is the much higher false positive rate, which means, that more non-swarms are confused with swarms. This means the additional measurements introduce more noise as would be necessary for predicting swarms. As shown in Fig. 8, adjacent sensors correlate strongly within the normal data, thus they bear no additional information during training, but weaker so within the anomaly set. Only including new sources of information (like the scale) would help in the multivariate sensor setting, as shown in Figs. 6a and 6b.

6.3 Methodology

In Sect. 3 we described our empirically founded, but manual approach of splitting data into anomalous behavior and normal sensor data. However, this data splitting method is ambiguous and highly susceptible to missing days in the corresponding dataset, i.e. missing anomalies and therefore mislabeling specific days. A general, rule-based approach of splitting anomalous and normal data, i.e. all windows with sensor values drifting for more than two standard deviations, doesn't work, since it removes most swarming events from the test set. A clearer split of training and testing data can only be ensured by very thorough labeling of the sensor values, which has to be done on different sensors independently.

In this work we evaluated predictions in an automated manner by using a random search for the best parameter settings (Table 4) using only labelled information of swarming events. In previous work [6] we selected the parameter α for the AE for detecting anomalies manually. This is a first step towards the automation of the anomaly detectors, but still has the problem of only being optimized for one anomaly class and still results in false positives for swarming events, but true positives for other anomalies.

Summarizing the results, the AE is the best all purpose swarm detector within the machine learning algorithms. It is out-performed to RBA for swarming detection, but it is also capable of predicting other anomalies without the knowledge of special rules.

7   Analysis

In this section we analyze the found anomalies and will outline different types of anomalies reported by the AE. We used this model exemplary to show interesting observations from the predictions, not only focussing on swarms, but also the aforementioned false positives, as well as true positives for other anomalies, hidden from the above discussion.

Swarming Events. All swarming events predicted with temperature sensors T_6 and T_m by the AE and RBA can be found in Table 3. Events observed by apiarists on site are marked with *. This table lists all swarm like events detected by RBA, as well as additionally missed swarming events. In other words, we used RBA to verify the results of the AE and vice versa, as described in [6]. Figure 5 shows a sensor data plot for a prototypical swarm for the hive in Bad Schwartau. Swarming events can be found within the table as *location (S)*, whereas other anomalies are denoted with *location (O)*. A more detailed view of the findings regarding swarming events is given in [6].

Table 3. Detected Anomalies. The first column shows the shortened name of the used test (anomaly) set (B. S. is Bad Schwartau, Wü. is Würzburg, Jel. is Jelgava, M. I. is Markt Indersdorf). (S) signifies that the set contains swarms while (O) stands for other anomalies. The next column displays the date of the event, and—where suitable—a reference to figures in the text. The last two columns indicate whether RBA or our method (AE) detected the anomaly. Predictions on HOBOS-hives are based on sensor T_6, on T_m for we4bee. We used the Bad Schwartau trained model to predict the swarms in any other beehive, except for Bad Schwartau itself [6].

Dataset	Timestamp	Detected		Dataset	Timestamp	Detected	
		RBA	AE			RBA	AE
	2016-05-11 11:05[5]	✓	✓		2015-05-06 18:02*	✓	✓
	2016-05-22 07:30	✓	✓		2016-06-02 13:48*	✓	✓
	2017-06-06 15:02	✓	✓		2016-05-30 10:03*	✓	✓
B. S. (S)	2019-05-13 09:30*	✓	✓		2016-06-16 15:50*	✓	✓
	2019-05-21 09:15*	✓	✓	Jel. (S)	2016-06-01 13:20*	✓	✓
	2019-05-25 12:00*	✓	✓		2016-06-03 09:11*	✓	✓
B. S. (O)	2016-08-03 17:24	✓	✓		2016-06-13 03:30	✓	✓
					2016-06-16 10:52*	✓	✓
Wü. (S)	2019-05-01 09:15[6a]		✓		2016-06-13 13:32*	✓	✓
	2019-05-10 11:15[6b]	✓	✓				
Wü. (O)	2019-04-17 16:22[6c]	✓	✓	M. I. (O)	2019-07-26 08:10	✓	✓
					2019-08-31 17:08[7b]		✓

Other Anomalies. Figure 6 depicts anomalies easily confused with swarms in at least one sensor. Figure 7 on the other hand, show anomalies categorized as external interference. They all display the same sensors, two temperature sensors (HOBOS: T_6, T_8; we4bee: T_r, T_m) and the weight on the scale. An exemplary plot of a training sample can be seen in Fig. 3. Sensors in Fig. 5 show the expected behavior for a swarming event, as already stated in Sect. 5.

Detecting swarms only in traces of temperature data, also has its drawbacks, as Fig. 6c shows, since the values of the weight sensors tend to describe normal behavior, whereas the temperature sensors follow the expected inverted parabola.

Similar implications can be seen in Fig. 6b, as a slice of the window actually contains a swarm, shown by all three sensors, whereas a later slice only indicates a swarm temperature-wise.

Figure 6a shows a swarming event, which RBA only detects in T_8, but not T_6, since it is not covered by the defined rules for swarms. The AE on the other hand is capable of detecting this swarm in both temperature sensors.

Figure 7a depicts the sensor traces of an opened apiary, which becomes obvious in the fast and strong drop in weight, and with varying delay in time, in the temperature sensors. This is due to the influx of ambient air, cooling the temperature within the beehive. As soon as the hive is closed the expected values, the same as before opening, are reported again.

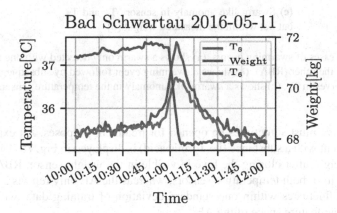

Fig. 5. (Prototypical) Swarm as indicated by T_6 and T_8, detected by RBA and AE [6].

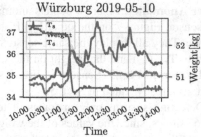

(a) Swarm detected with T_8, but not with T_6 (RBA). Anomaly in both for AE. Swarm anomaly within the weight.[6]

(b) Swarm anomaly indicated by both T_6 and T_8, but additional swarms in T_8. Swarm anomaly within the weight.[6]

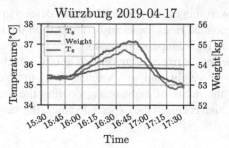

(c) Swarm-like anomaly in sensors T_6 and T_8, but not within the measured weight.[6]

Fig. 6. Special cases of swarming events. (a) shows a swarm only detected with one temperature sensor, but not the other (RBA). (b) shows a swarming event followed by subsequent swam-like temperature curves in T_8. (c) shows a swarm-like anomaly in the temperature sensors, but not in the scale.

The beehive must sometimes be opened for treatment purposes. An example of a varroa treatment with a substance (i.e. formic acid) is displayed in Fig. 7b. The resulting additional weight after closing the hive in visible in the weight sensor. RBA confuses this as a swarm in both temperature sensors, whereas the AE only reports a swarm for T_r. T_m only fluctuates within one standard deviation of training data, which can be captured by the feature space of the AE.

Aforementioned anomalies are only a subset of reported anomalies, since the AE detects a lot more. Some of them are not as easily classified, but normally are temperature values far lower than 30 °C. Even sensor anomalies are detected by AE, as can be seen in Fig. 7c.

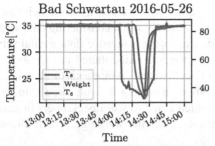

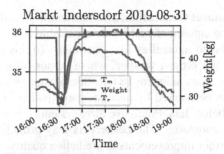

(a) External interference of an opened apiary. The influx of outer air leads to the temperature drop.[6]

(b) External interference by a possible varroa treatment. The beehive was opened, weight added, leading to the excitement of bees with a temperature increase. In contrast to our AE with T_m, RBA detected a swarm with T_r and T_m.[6]

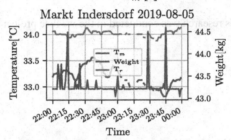

(c) Sensor anomaly with missing values in T_r and T_m, but not in the measured weights.[6]

Fig. 7. External interference anomalies. (a) shows an opened hive with no modifications, whereas (b) is opened for treatment with a substance added. (c) shows missing sensor values.

8 Conclusion/Future Work

In this work we evaluated the use of machine learning models for anomaly detection in beehives. We compared the models Elliptic Envelope, Isolation Forests, Local Outlier Factor, One-Class SVMs, and recurrent autoencoders quantitatively for swarm detection. The results show that the AE is the best multi-purpose anomaly detector in comparison. It is able to detect swarms with high accuracy even by only optimizing the decision threshold with very sparse swarm instances. Within the multivariate temperature sensor setting we found, that combining three sensors incurs more noise than information, and still needs further experiments and evaluation. Especially combining different sensor types, i.e. temperature and weight, seems to be more promising. Multiple aspects of anomaly detection in beehives require more work in the future:

Evaluation of Deep Generative Models. Other types of deep neural networks will have to be explored in future work. For example, generative models like variational autoencoders or generative adversarial networks show particular promise, since they have two advantages: A) anomalies may exist within the training set, and B) they allow for probability-based classification instead of relying solely on the reconstruction error [1].

Dataset Generation. Machine learning models require data to correctly learn their task. The amount of beehive data available is limited, especially when considering data with labeled anomalies like swarming. To this end, we hope to improve data availability in the project we4bee, where sensor-equipped apiaries are distributed mostly across Germany, allowing us to collect a large dataset of beehive data. Any events or anomalies can be marked by apiarists participating in we4bee, providing us with more valuable labeled data. Predictive alert-systems can be implemented to warn beekeepers in case of anomalies. The beekeepers may provide feedback for the warnings, which allows further improvements in prediction quality.

Winter Period. During winter, bees enter a passive state where their behavior changes significantly in comparison to summer time [24]. To learn normal behavior of bees for their active summer time, we excluded data from October through March for all datasets (cf. Sect. 3). Detecting anomalies during winter can also be of interest but this remains future work.

Acknowledgements. This research was conducted in the we4bee project sponsored by the Audi Environmental Foundation.

Appendix

Sensor Correlations

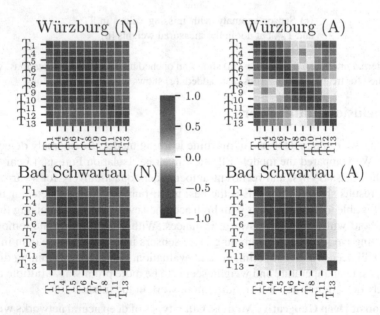

Fig. 8. Sensor correlations. All figures display the Pearson correlation between temperature sensors within a given beehive. (N) stands for the dataset containing normal behavior and (A) for the dataset with anomalous behavior [6].

Hyperparameters

Table 4. Optimized parameters and their ranges for the anomaly detectors within the random search. $\mathcal{U}_x$ describes an uniform distribution with $[0, x)$, whereas $\mathcal{I}_{a,b}$ represents a random integer distribution with $[a, b]$. $\mathcal{LU}_{a,b}$ is a log uniform distribution with parameters a, b.

Classifier	Hyperparameter	Range
Local Outlier Factor	n neighbors	$\mathcal{I}_{1,100}$
	algorithm	ball tree, kd tree
	leaf size	$\mathcal{I}_{1,150}$
	contamination	$\mathcal{U}_{0.5}$
	metric	chebyshev, cityblock, euclidean, infinity, l1, l2, manhattan, minkowski
Elliptic Envelope	assume centered	True, False
	support fraction	$\mathcal{U}_1$
	contamination	$\mathcal{U}_{0.5}$
Isolation Forest	n estimators	$\mathcal{I}_{10,100}$
	max samples	auto
	contamination	$\mathcal{U}_{0.5}$
	max features	$\mathcal{U}_1$
	bootstrap	True, False
One- Class SVM	kernel	linear, poly(degree=3), rbf(coef0=0), sigmoid
	shrinking	True, False
	γ	$\mathcal{LU}_{0.0001,1}$
	ν	$\mathcal{LU}_{0.0001,1}$
AE	hidden size	$\mathcal{I}_{2,64}$
	layers	$\mathcal{I}_{1,4}$

References

1. An, J., Cho, S.: Variational autoencoder based anomaly detection using reconstruction probability. Special Lecture IE **2**(1) (2015)
2. Bergstra, J., Bengio, Y.: Random search for hyper-parameter optimization. J. Mach. Learn. Res. **13**, 281–305 (2012)
3. Breunig, M.M., Kriegel, H.P., Ng, R.T., Sander, J.: LOF: identifying density-based local outliers. In: Proceedings of the 2000 ACM SIGMOD International Conference on Management of Data, pp. 93–104 (2000)
4. Chalapathy, R., Chawla, S.: Deep learning for anomaly detection: a survey. CoRR abs/1901.03407 (2019). http://arxiv.org/abs/1901.03407
5. Cortes, C., Vapnik, V.: Support-vector networks. Mach. Learn. **20**(3), 273–297 (1995). https://doi.org/10.1007/BF00994018
6. Davidson, P., Steininger, M., Lautenschlager, F., Kobs, K., Krause, A., Hotho, A.: Anomaly detection in beehives using deep recurrent autoencoders. In: Proceedings of the 9th International Conference on Sensor Networks (SENSORNETS 2020), pp. 142–149. No. 9, SCITEPRESS - Science and Technology Publications, LDA (2020)
7. Fell, R., et al.: The seasonal cycle of swarming in honeybees. J. Apic. Res. **16**(4), 170–173 (1977)

8. Ferrari, S., Silva, M., Guarino, M., Berckmans, D.: Monitoring of swarming sounds in bee hives for early detection of the swarming period. Comput. Electron. Agric. **64**(1), 72–77 (2008)
9. Filonov, P., Lavrentyev, A., Vorontsov, A.: Multivariate industrial time series with cyber-attack simulation: fault detection using an LSTM-based predictive data model. In: NIPS Time Series Workshop 2016 (2016)
10. Kingma, D.P., Ba, J.: Adam: A method for stochastic optimization. arXiv preprint arXiv:1412.6980 (2014)
11. Kridi, D.S., Carvalho, C.G.N.d., Gomes, D.G.: A predictive algorithm for mitigate swarming bees through proactive monitoring via wireless sensor networks. In: Proceedings of the 11th ACM Symposium on PE-WASUN, pp. 41–47. ACM (2014)
12. Li, K.L., Huang, H.K., Tian, S.F., Xu, W.: Improving one-class SVM for anomaly detection. In: Proceedings of the 2003 International Conference on Machine Learning and Cybernetics (IEEE Cat. No. 03EX693), vol. 5, pp. 3077–3081. IEEE (2003)
13. Liu, F.T., Ting, K.M., Zhou, Z.H.: Isolation forest. In: 2008 Eighth IEEE International Conference on Data Mining, pp. 413–422. IEEE (2008)
14. Liu, F.T., Ting, K.M., Zhou, Z.H.: Isolation-based anomaly detection. ACM Trans. Knowl. Discov. Data **6**(1), 1–39 (2012)
15. Malhotra, P., et al.: Multi-sensor prognostics using an unsupervised health index based on LSTM encoder-decoder. In: 1st SIGKDD Workshop on ML for PHM, August 2016
16. Malhotra, P., Ramakrishnan, A., Anand, G., Vig, L., Agarwal, P., Shroff, G.: LSTM-based encoder-decoder for multi-sensor anomaly detection. arXiv preprint arXiv:1607.00148 (2016)
17. Pedregosa, F., et al.: Scikit-learn: machine learning in python. J. Mach. Learn. Res. **12**, 2825–2830 (2011)
18. Rousseeuw, P.J.: Least median of squares regression. J. Am. Stat. Assoc. **79**(388), 871–880 (1984)
19. Rousseeuw, P.J., Driessen, K.V.: A fast algorithm for the minimum covariance determinant estimator. Technometrics **41**(3), 212–223 (1999)
20. Ryan, J., Lin, M.J., Miikkulainen, R.: Intrusion detection with neural networks. In: Advances in Neural Information Processing Systems, pp. 943–949 (1998)
21. Schölkopf, B., Platt, J.C., Shawe-Taylor, J., Smola, A.J., Williamson, R.C.: Estimating the support of a high-dimensional distribution. Neural Comput. **13**(7), 1443–1471 (2001)
22. Shipmon, D.T., Gurevitch, J.M., Piselli, P.M., Edwards, S.T.: Time series anomaly detection; detection of anomalous drops with limited features and sparse examples in noisy highly periodic data. arXiv preprint arXiv:1708.03665 (2017)
23. Winston, M.: Swarming, afterswarming, and reproductive rate of unmanaged honeybee colonies (apis mellifera). Insectes Soc. **27**(4), 391–398 (1980)
24. Zacepins, A., Brusbardis, V., Meitalovs, J., Stalidzans, E.: Challenges in the development of precision beekeeping. Biosys. Eng. **130**, 60–71 (2015)
25. Zacepins, A., Kviesis, A., Stalidzans, E., Liepniece, M., Meitalovs, J.: Remote detection of the swarming of honey bee colonies by single-point temperature monitoring. Biosys. Eng. **148**, 76–80 (2016)
26. Zhou, C., Paffenroth, R.C.: Anomaly detection with robust deep autoencoders. In: Proceedings of the 23rd ACM SIGKDD, pp. 665–674. ACM (2017)
27. Zhu, X., Wen, X., Zhou, S., Xu, X., Zhou, L., Zhou, B.: The temperature increase at one position in the colony can predict honey bee swarming (apis cerana). J. Apic. Res. **58**(4), 489–491 (2019)

Evaluation of a CDM Interrogation Scheme Allowing Spectrally Overlapping FBG Sensors

Marek Götten[1,2(✉)] [iD], Steffen Lochmann[1] [iD], Andreas Ahrens[1] [iD], and César Benavente-Peces[2] [iD]

[1] Bereich Elektrotechnik und Informatik, Hochschule Wismar, Philipp-Müller-Straße 14, 23966 Wismar, Germany
{marek.goetten,steffen.lochmann,andreas.ahrens}@hs-wismar.de
[2] Escuela Técnica Superior de Ingenería y Sistemas de Telecomunicación, Universidad Politécnica de Madrid, Crtra de Valenica, km 7, Madrid, Spain
cesar.benavente@upm.es
https://www.hs-wismar.de/, https://www.etsist.upm.es/

Abstract. This contribution evaluates the potential of a code-division multiplex (CDM) interrogated fiber optical sensor network, namely a fiber-Bragg grating (FBG) sensor network. The basic principle is briefly outlined and a detailed analysis on trigger schemes is performed. It focuses on the impact on the autocorrelation function of a predetermined orthogonal code. For limit assessments, a modified signal to multi user interference (MUI) ratio mSMUI is introduced which can be applied to a CDM interrogated sensing network, as well as to a wavelengthdivision multiplex (WDM) interrogation. A trigger scheme which realizes a code delay with rotated codes and adds a zero padding to fill the integration time without truncating codes turns out of to be the best suitable trigger scheme in terms of mSMUI. Based on typical hardware parameters, a theoretical capacity limit of a CDM interrogation system is estimated to 376 sensors with overlapping spectra. A mSMUI measurement in a sensor network testbed proves the practical operation of the system. A comparison of CDM and WDM in terms of the mSMUI shows ratios of 21.41 dB for CDM in contrary to 12.43 dB for WDM, even when the practical peak height of sensors in the spectrum reached only up to 70% of the theoretical height. At the end, a hybrid scheme containing a combination of CDM and WDM is shown which is able to interrogate 2000 serial FBGs.

Keywords: Fiber-Bragg-Gratings (FBGs) · Code-Division Multiplex (CDM) · Serial sensor networks · Smart structures

1 Introduction

The interest in optical fiber sensors and sensor networks has increased tremendously in the last years. The inherit advantages, such as electro-magenetic interference (EMI) resistance, small size and weight or immunity to hazardous environments, make these sensors the equipment of choice in a lot of applications

© Springer Nature Switzerland AG 2022
A. Ahrens et al. (Eds.): SENSORNETS 2020/2021, CCIS 1674, pp. 21–38, 2022.
https://doi.org/10.1007/978-3-031-17718-7_2

[18]. They can be found in rail system surveillance [4], availability checks of passive optical networks [5,19] or in the medical field, for example temperature monitoring in cancer treatments [12]. In terms of smart-structures or structural health monitoring [3,11,17] the multiplexing capability of fiber-Bragg gratings (FBGs) gains particular interests. A typical multiplexing scheme is wavelength-divisionmultiplex (WDM) [7], where sensors share a broadband spectrum to operate at different Bragg-wavelengths. It is limited to the spectral width of the light source or the detector. Time-division mutliplex (TDM) makes use of different propagation times of short light pulses to overcome the spectral limitations. Reflected light from FBGs at different locations in a fiber arrives with a distinct time delay at the detector. Thus, it can be matched to the corresponding sensor [20,23]. Another approach makes use of optical frequency domain refractometry (OFDR) to interrogate identical serial sensors by means of an in-fiber interferometer [6,13]. Frequency shifted interferometry (FSI) showed interesting results in large fiber optical sensor networks [16] as well.

This work analyzes another multiplexing scheme, called code-division multiplex (CDM). It relies on reflected codes with different arrival times due to different optical path lengths, similar to TDM. Applying orthogonal codes, the interference of neighboring sensors is canceled out, so that overlapping FBG spectra are allowed. It should not be confused with spectral CDM [22], where FBG spectra are designed with regards to orthogonal codes. Unlike using a single short light pulse to interrogate sensors, CDM uses a chain of light pulses that form a code. Therefore, a better signal-to-noiseratio (SNR) is obtained compared to TDM. Furthermore, there are only a few network configuration restrictions compared to OFDR. Additionally, the spectral information of FBGs is measured by the spectrometer and is not found in a rather unstable amplitude measurement as for FSI.

This contribution is a revision and extension of results published in [10]. The remaining part of this work is structured as follows: In Sect. 2 the theory of a CDM interrogation scheme is outlined. Section 3 provides an in-depth evaluation of different trigger schemes with respect to [10]. These schemes have an impact on the autocorrelation function (ACF) which is an important parameter in a CDM system. In addition to [10], Sect. 4 proposes a theoretical limit of such an interrogation scheme. Furthermore, Sect. 5 provides measurements carried out in the CDM interrogator testbed. In Sect. 6 an introduction to a hybrid CDM-WDM system can be found. Section 7 concludes the work.

2   Theory of CDM Interrogation and Testbed Implementation

The multiplexing technique CDM is based on orthogonal codes and derived from data transmission systems [14]. Each sensor in a serial fiber-optical network can operate at the same wavelength but can still be addressed individually. The interrogation system makes use of different propagation times from the first modulator to each sensor and back to the second modulator. Reflected light from sensors further to the end of the network arrives later at the second modulator. When a code is applied to the light traveling to the end of the network, a set of reflected codes, each with a distinct arrival time, reaches the second modulator. There, all arriving codes are modulated with the same code shifted in time. This corresponds to a multiplication of two codes. After the modulation process, the remaining light is collected by a spectrometer. Multiplication and summation represent a correlation with the same code. The second modulator needs to be synchronized to a desired reflected code. This correlation process corresponds to the autocorrelation peak. All non-synchronized codes form the sidelobes of the ACF. A superposition of the autocorrelation peak with all sidelobes takes place in the spectrometer. To obtain only the light of a specified sensor, all sidelobes need to be as low as possible, meaning, no light of non-synchronized codes should pass the second modulator and interfere with the synchronized code light. This interrogation procedure leads to a unipolar-unipolar autocorrelation process. By nature, interference passing the second modulator can only add up. A second correlation step, where the second modulator is driven with the inverted code, is introduced. This procedure is called sequence inverse keying (SIK) [2,9,15]. The second acquired spectrum is subtracted from the first one. The autocorrelation turns into a unipolar-bipolar correlation with better orthogonality than a single correlation step [8]. The implementation in a testbed is shown in Fig. 1. A superluminiscent light emitting diode (SLD) provides a broadband spectrum for the FBG in the network. The broadband light is switched on and off according to a code applied by modulator I. The electrical signal for the modulation process comes from the pattern generator. The modulated light travels through the circulator and reaches the network. Each FBG reflects the code at the same wavelength. But different locations of each FBG introduce propagation delays between each code. The reflected codes pass the circulator again and reach the modulator through a polarization controller. It is used to optimize the modulation result as it is polarization dependent. Modulator II is driven by an electrical signal out of channel 1 of the pattern generator. This signal can be delayed by Δt so that it is synchronized to a specific reflected code. The output of the second modulator is collected by the spectrometer during a specified integration time. To obtain a modulation process only during an acquisition of a spectrum, the spectrometer emits a trigger signal. The pattern generator can react to this trigger. A second modulation step takes place while

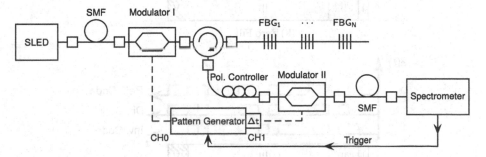

Fig. 1. Implementation of the CDM interrogator system with a serial network of 25 FBGs operating at the same wavelength.

the second modulator is driving with the inverted code, so that SIK is performed. Further details can be found in [1,9].

3   Trigger Schemes for the CDM Interrogator and Their Influence on Autocorrelation Functions

3.1   Trigger Schemes

The communication between the components of the testbed is controlled by a trigger signal. Namely, the spectrometer triggers the data generator to start with its output of the code that consists out of several chips. Chips can be either a logical '0' or a logical '1'. The modulators switch according to this code signal. The two serial correlation processes, direct and inverted, differ in the code signal applied to the second modulator. When the acquisition of a spectrum starts, the spectrometer sends a rising voltage edge and when it ends, a falling edge. The behavior of the codes at the second modulator is depicted in Fig. 2. Three

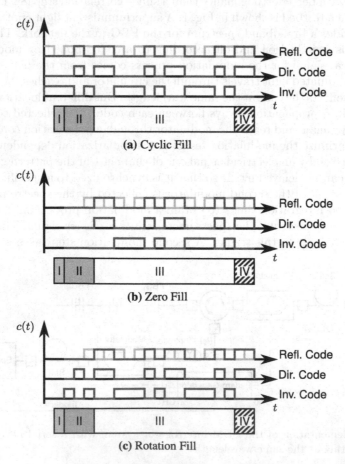

Fig. 2. Phases of trigger scheme.

possibilities of the code behavior are shown in the diagrams; Cyclic Fill, Zero Fill and Rotation Fill. In this work, the applied code has a length of 131 chips and shows good characteristics for the CDM interrogation system. The acquisition of a spectrum can be divided into four phases (I–IV). Phase I is referred to as *trigger delay phase* and stands for the time delay from emitting the trigger signal until starting with the switching process of the modulators. This is mainly caused by electrical cables and internal circuits and currently in the order of 40 ns. The second phase, namely *code delay phase*, describes the time period, during which earlier reflected codes arrive at the second modulator. Phase III is the *synchronization phase*, where the reflected code and the second modulator are synchronized. Ideally, the switching of the modulator is equal to the reflected code pattern. The last phase IV is called *truncation phase*. Once the integration time ends, the spectrometer does not acquire any light although the switching process is not yet finished. The rest of the code is basically truncated [10].

The Cyclic Fill, shown in Fig. 2a, is not dependent on a trigger, since the codes are repeated continuously. The spectrometer's integration starts at a certain point and ends after a specified time period. Ideally, the integration time is equal to a multiple of the code length, so that a cyclic autocorrelation is realized. Phase I, II and IV do not affect the modulators driving signal. The data generator runs independently of the spectrometer. The whole integration time is filled with the correlation of two repeated codes.

The Zero Fill in Fig. 2b requires the trigger control. Therefore, both modulators are set to a logical '0' before the code output. In phase II, the first modulator starts switching and sends out the code that is reflected multiple times. The second modulator is synchronized to a specific reflected code and the delay is realized by filling phase II with logical '0's. The desired reflected code arrives and the switching according to the code begins in phase III, the *synchronization phase*. The end of the integration time (last part of phase III) can either be filled with parts of the code that is truncated in phase IV or it is filled with logical '0's and phase IV is skipped.

The Rotation Fill, depicted in Fig. 2c works similar to the Zero Fill. The main difference is that the *code delay phase* is not filled with logical '0's but with the last chips of the code. The delay is realized by rotating the code instead of shifting.

To analyze the impact of different triggering schemes, a criterion describing the quality of the codes is defined. A modified signal to multi user interference (MUI) ratio

$$\text{mSMUI} = \frac{S - \sum |MUI^-|}{N + \sum MUI^+} \tag{1}$$

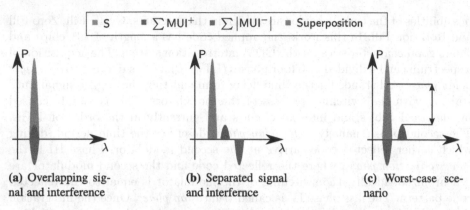

Fig. 3. Spectral scenarios for the definition of the worst-case criterion mSMUI.

is introduced based on CDM-interrogated fiber optical sensor networks. The parameter S stands for the signal amplitude of the interrogated sensor. It corresponds to the ACF peak at $\psi(\tau = 0)$. $\sum MUI^+$ stands for all positive sidelobes and $\sum |MUI^-|$ for all negative sidelobes. Interfering FBG sensors can move spectrally by applying strain or temperature. In Fig. 3a the spectral position of overlapping signal and MUI and its resulting superposition is depicted. The superposition is a result of $S + \sum MUI^+ + \sum |MUI^-|$. Theoretically, each single sensor is part of the MUI. But in the worst-case, all positive MUI and all negative MUI need to be treated separately. Figure 3b shows a separation of all three parts. The superposition on the wavelength range of the signal FBG results in the signal S itself. The signal amplitude is the maximum amplitude in the spectrum. The worst-case scenario is demonstrated in Fig. 3c, where the signal amplitude is diminished by all negative MUI. The peak detection of the signal is now in competition with all positive MUI. The ratio between the diminished signal and the positive MUI is the worst-case criterion mSMUI. Additionally, the noise of the spectrum is added to the positive MUI. This scenario is one out of a million possibilities so that most scenarios result in a better signal to MUI ratio. For all simulations, the noise is set to zero.

As an advantage, this worst-case criterion can be applied to a WDM sensor system, too. Since no MUI occurs, it is set to zero, and the result is an SNR.

3.2   Influence of Integration Time and Truncated Codes

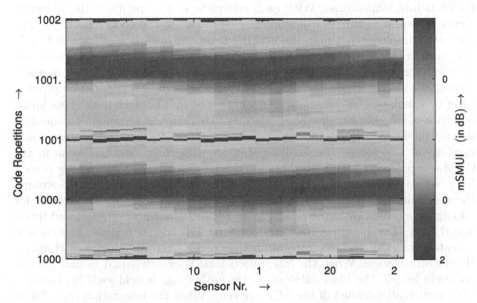

Fig. 4. The mSMUI according to Eq. 3.1 for 25 sensors and different integration times using Cyclic Fill. Code length equals 131 chips.

Figure 4 shows an example of the criterion mSMUI for 25 sensors in a network with a Cyclic Fill trigger scheme. The integration time is increased chip-wise to see the influence of all four phases, for example, if the code does not fit completely in the integration time and is truncated instead. The integration time is

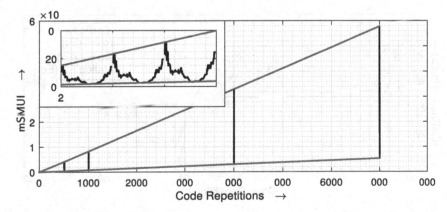

Fig. 5. Linear extrapolation of mSMUI for Cyclic Fill. The inset shows a zoom of the first code repetitions.

represented by non-integer multiples of the code length. Hence, a lot of different constellations need to be taken into account. Each sensor has a different mSMUI for each integration time. With each complete code repetition, the behavior seems to repeat. There is a periodical pattern along the code repetition axis. For each complete repetition, the mSMUI increases linearly as shown in Fig. 5. The inset in this figure shows two lines connecting all non-infinite maximum and all minimum values. It is a linear connection that can be extrapolated to a few thousand code repetitions necessary for typical integration times. The proof is done by simulating intermediate steps, indicated by the black lines. This linear behavior is suitable for all trigger schemes. Therefore, it is enough to simulate shorter integration times and estimate the outcome for long integration times used in the real setup. The analysis of codes with their autocorrelation in the CDM-setup can be done with short integration times to safe computing power. Each sensor has a different mSMUI for a certain integration time. Therefore, the minimum mSMUI out of 25 sensors is taken into account. The results for all trigger schemes are depicted in Fig. 6. Phase I is for now omitted and introduced later. The blue line indicates a Cyclic Fill trigger regime. The code is repeated endlessly and the integration time picks a certain amount of chips for the autocorrelation. When the integration time is exactly equal to multiples of the code length, the ideal value of ∞ for $mSMUI_{min}$ is achieved. No interference occurs, all sidelobes of the ACF are zero. When the integration time differs from an exact multiple of the code, the criterion collapses by up to $\sim$10 dB. The worst-case scenario is when half a code is truncated in phase IV. The testbed spectrometer uses integration times of a few milliseconds. The accuracy of the integration time can be doubted in relation to a chip length of a few nanoseconds. Therefore, the whole range between multiples of code lengths needs to be taken into account to determine a suitable trigger scheme. In general, filling the last phase of the integration time with parts of the code results in comparably low mSMUI. Zero Fill with code at the end (Ec) and Rotation Fill with code

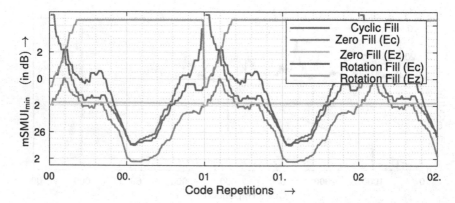

Fig. 6. Comparison of trigger regimes using the example of 500 to 502 code repetitions and the minimum mSMUI value out of 25 sensors. (Color figure online)

at the end (Ec) collapse as well, while logical '0's at the end (Ez) result in a steady criteria. Hence, the scheme Rotation Fill with a zero padding provides the best criterion behavior over a range of integration times. It is important to have an integration time that is long enough to cover also the last arriving codes. Therefore, not exactly multiples of the code result in a good criterion, but an integration time which is at least 20% longer. This corresponds to 25 Chips out of a code length of 131 Chips.

3.3   Influence of Leading Trigger Delays

Phase IV has now been analyzed by adding zeros or parts of the code. Simulations show the best criterion for complete codes within the integration time. Phase I which has been omitted so far, is now analyzed in the following. This phase is a result of communication delays between starting the integration time and the arrival of the first reflected code at the second modulator. Technically, it is impossible to skip this phase when a trigger mechanism is applied, so that different delays are analyzed. In Fig. 7 the influence of different trigger delays is depicted. The $mSMUI_{min}$ is chosen out of 25 sensors and all integration times between 500 and 501 times the code length. This leads to a worst-case criterion depending only on the trigger delay. When no trigger delay occurs, the worst-case results match with the previous discussions. Increasing the delay can result in truncating codes in phase IV. This leads to worse $mSMUI_{min}$ values. Therefore, both zero padding schemes collapse with higher trigger delays. Both code endings do not explicitly depend on the trigger delay, since the scheme itself contains a truncation of the code. Cyclic Fill has a slightly increasing $mSMUI_{min}$ value but does not reach the decreasing zero padding schemes. The trigger delay is shown for practical relevant values. Measurements have shown, that a trigger delay of ~40 ns can be expected which is equivalent to 20 Chips at a chip rate of 200 MChips/s. For lower chip rates, the equivalent amount of chips for such a trigger delay decreases. Therefore, the trigger scheme Rotation Fill with logical '0's at the end remains the best scheme. Moreover, the graph on the right depicts the influence of the shift on the decreasing $mSMUI_{min}$. For no shift, the integration time should be long enough to cover the last reflected code (here 25 chips later which correspond to 20% of the code). The axis *Part of Code* indicates the additional length of the integration time in relation to the first reflected code. 0% indicates an integration time that ends immediately with the end of the first code. Hence all other reflected codes are truncated. This can be seen in the low $mSMUI_{min}$. To cover the last reflected code completely, that arrives 25 Chips later, the integration time needs to be 25 chips longer which corresponds to ~20% of the code. Then the criterion is stable. Increasing the trigger delay shifts this limit further apart. For a delay of 60 chips, the integration time should be 25 Chips + 60 Chips = 85 Chips $\hat{=}$ 64%. For longer integration times the criterion remains stable. Hence, every trigger delay can be compensated with a longer integration time. The main goal is to not truncate a code and change its autocorrelation properties.

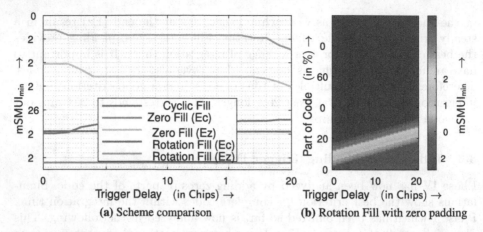

Fig. 7. Influence of trigger delay phase. Code length equals 131 Chips and the minimum mSMUI$_{min}$ is depicted. In b) the increased integration time is represented as a percentage of the code length.

3.4 Influence of Non-ideal Modulation Coefficients

Another analysis focuses on the modulation coefficients. To switch light on and off according to a code, electro-optic modulators (EOMs) are implemented in the testbed. Ideal modulation stands for modulation coefficients of 1 and 0. For a logical '1', the light is not attenuated, hence multiplied by 1. A logical '0' blocks all incoming light, thus multiplied by 0. The modulation coefficients are $\alpha_0, \alpha_1, \beta_0, \beta_1$. The first modulator is described with the α-coefficients and the second one with the β-coefficients. Logical '1' '0' is indicated by the index.

In Fig. 8 the influence of non-ideal modulation coefficients is shown for Cyclic Fill, Zero Fill and Rotation Fill, the last two with zero padding. Only one modulation coefficient has an influence on the criterion that is α_0, which is the light blocking capability of the first modulator. This has also been shown in [8]. All other coefficients influence the autocorrelation in a scaling manner. The ratio between sidelobes and autocorrelation peak remains stable so that the criterion remains stable as well. This applies to all trigger schemes equally.

Summarizing this Sect. 3, different trigger schemes have been analyzed in a simulation of the testbed. Different parameters have been taken into account and the result is a trigger scheme called, Rotation Fill with zero padding. The criterion provides optimal results for all influences analyzed.

4   Theoretical Limit of a CDM Interrogation System

The maximum peak height of an FBG in a difference spectrum depends on the capacity of the implemented charge-coupled device (CCD) spectrometer. Each pixel can collect a certain amount of light that is converted into Counts. The maximum amount of Counts per pixel C defines the resolution of the spectrum

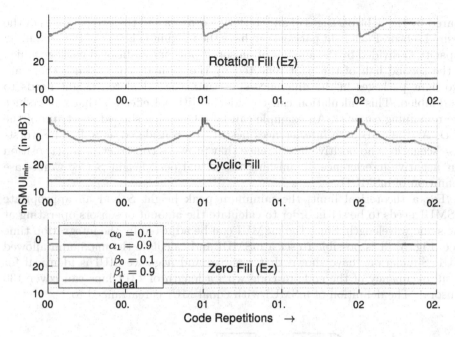

Fig. 8. Influence of non-ideal modulation coefficients on different trigger schemes. Each time, only one parameter is changed and the rest is kept ideal. α: first modulator, β: second modulator.

for further signal processing. The introduced CDM interrogation scheme uses SIK to demultiplex the serial sensors. The outcome is a difference spectrum due to the subtraction of two acquired spectra. The SIK process is depicted in Fig. 9. To obtain an ideal difference spectrum, the interference needs to be canceled out. Since the difference spectrum is the result of a subtraction of two spectra, the interference has to be equally distributed between both spectra. This is done by the applied code in the second modulation process. Positive interference is part of the direct spectrum and negative interference must be part of the inverted spectrum. The light of each sensor can be considered as two small packages of light which are ideally distributed equally to the direct and the inverted spectrum. This separation takes place for all interference sensors (FBG 0 to $I-2$). Only the light packages of the desired sensor, the modulator is synchronized to, should be part of the direct spectrum. Therefore, both light packages can be found in the direct spectrum. Additionally, the noise is added to both spectra, as well as the corresponding interference package. Subtracting both spectra, all interference that is distributed equally, disappears. The mean value of the noise $\overline{N}$ cancels out as well. The light of the desired sensor remains in the difference spectrum and the standard deviation $\sigma(N)$ of both spectra overlap. The positive interference is added and the negative interference is subtracted. The height S can be calculated. The capacity C is diminished by the noise's mean and standard deviation as well as the positive interference. The remaining part is shared by the light packages of all interfering sensors and the two packages of the desired sensor. Each light package can have the maximum height of the remaining capacity C divided by the amount of sensors I plus one additional package which is the second half of the light reflected by the desired sensor. Since there are two light packages in the difference spectrum, the calculated height needs to be doubled. This calculation can consider additional effects ϵ that can reduce the remaining capacity. An example can be a Gaussian shaped spectrum of the SLD. At the end, both interferences need to be considered as well. The worst-case scenario is no positive interference that provides constructive superposition but negative interference diminishing the actual peak height S (see worst-case definition of mSMUI).

For a theoretical limit, the minimum peak height S and an appropriate mSMUI needs to be set in order to calculate the amount of sensors operating at the same wavelength. Since the mSMUI can be adjusted by the integration time (see. Fig. 5), it is possible to set a mSMUI and calculate the maximum allowed MUI. Simulations have shown that positive and negative MUI is identical for a full occupancy of the code (a code with a length of 131 Chips can cover 130 sensors). The definition of mSMUI with equal MUI is rearranged to

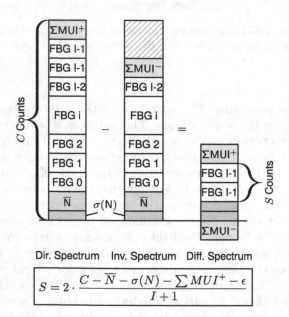

$$S = 2 \cdot \frac{C - \overline{N} - \sigma(N) - \sum MUI^+ - \epsilon}{I+1}$$

Fig. 9. Spectral influences of the CDM approach with SIK. (Color figure online)

Table 1. Parameters for a theoretical limit of used testbed.

Parameter	Value (in counts)	Description
C	60000	Maximum usable capacity of spectrometer
$\overline{N}$	3379	Mean of noise
$\sigma(N)$	10	Standard deviation of noise
ϵ	0	Other influences
S	150	Minimum detectable peak height
mSMUI	3	Appropriate ratio

$$\sum MUI^+ = \sum |MUI^-| = \frac{S - \text{mSMUI} \cdot N}{\text{mSMUI} + 1} \overset{!}{\geq} 0. \tag{2}$$

It needs to be denoted that $\sum MUI^+$ by definition cannot be negative. The mSMUI cannot be smaller than the remaining SNR without any MUI. The noise N in Eq. 2 corresponds to the noise in the difference spectrum and is hence set to $2 \times \sigma(N)$. To provide at least 3 sampling points for a peak in the spectrum the peak height should not be too small [21]. A low peak height results in pixels close to the noise which affects the curve fitting for peak detection. Therefore, a peak height of 150 Counts is chosen. The mSMUI is set to 3, so that the resulting peak height in the worst-case is 3 times the spectrally shifted MUI peak including noise. This results in a $\sum MUI^+$ equal to 23 Counts according to Eq. 2. The equation from Fig. 9 for the minimum peak height S can be rearranged to calculate an amount of sensors I

$$I \leq 2 \cdot \frac{C - \overline{N} - \sigma(N) - \sum MUI^+ - \epsilon}{S} - 1. \tag{3}$$

Inserting the parameters from Table 1 the theoretical limit of sensors operating at the same wavelength can be set to $I \leq 376$ sensors. This limitation is a result of the implemented spectrometer. The parameter ϵ is still set to zero. Assuming influences going up to half of the maximum capacity C, the limit of sensors decreases down to $I \leq 176$ sensors operating at the same wavelength.

5   SNR Comparison of CDM and WDM

This section deals with the comparison of a WDM system and the CDM system in terms of SNR. Since sensors in a WDM do not suffer from interferences, a single sensor represents this system. Whereas the CDM system is implemented with 25 sensors operating at the same wavelength. The testbed parameters are the same. The integration time is set to 7 ms and the peak height in the spectrometer is adjusted by an optical attenuator in front of the spectrometer. The depicted peaks are a result of a Gaussian approximation, to receive a proper peak height out of a few pixels of the spectrometer. The peak height in the direct spectrum

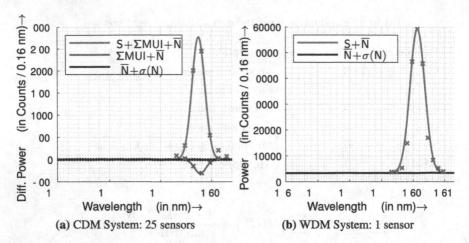

(a) CDM System: 25 sensors   **(b) WDM System: 1 sensor**

Fig. 10. Measurement taken with similar integration time and equivalent input intensity to compare the CDM system with 25 spectral overlapping sensors and a WDM system represented by a single sensor since no overlapping can occur. (Color figure online)

of the SIK procedure is set to ∼60000 Counts which nearly corresponds to the maximum capacity. The resulting peak in the difference spectrum is depicted in Fig. 10a. This peak is a superposition of signal peak, interference peaks (MUI) and noise. To measure the MUI, the signal peak is moved to higher wavelengths by applying strain to the corresponding sensor. The synchronization point is not changed, so that the interference gets visible. This peak is a superposition of all MUI and noise. When the network is not connected, the remaining signal in the difference spectrum corresponds to the noise of the system. The same result is obtained by applying the maximum attenuation of ∼60 dB.

This can be used to check the theoretical signal peak height S according to Sect. 4. The capacity C is set to 60000 Counts and the sum of the positive MUI is set to 0. The measurement in Fig. 10a only shows a sum of all interference. The theoretical value for S gets better with less positive MUI. Therefore, the best case of $\sum MUI^+ = 0$ is chosen. The noise parameters are kept identical as in Sect. 4. The result of the equation from Fig. 9 is $S = 4354$ Counts. In contrary, the measured signal peak height equals $2769\,textCounts + 313\,textCounts = 3082\,textCounts$, since the MUI (blue) needs to be deducted from the superposition indicated in red. Therefore, the measured peak height in the difference spectrum is approximately 70% of the theoretical peak height. The differences are mainly introduced by non-ideal modulation coefficients and need to be further analyzed.

The criterion of Sect. 3.1 can be applied here. Due to the practical setup it is not possible to separate the whole MUI. The blue curve depicts the superposition of all positive and negative interference which is negative in total. In this comparison therefore, the superposition of the whole MUI is taken into consideration. The red curve indicates already the diminished peak height by the superposition of the MUI. Hence, the numerator of the fraction equals the measurement which leads to

$$\mathrm{mSMUI_{CDM25}} = \frac{2769\,\mathrm{Counts}}{20\,\mathrm{Counts}} = 138.45 \,\hat{=}\, 21.41\,\mathrm{dB}. \qquad (4)$$

In Fig. 10b the results for a WDM system are depicted. The peak height is set to ~60000 Counts. No MUI can interfere with the signal peak. The noise of the system is obtained in the same way, by detaching the fiber containing the sensor from the interrogation system. The remaining signal is the noise that occurs in every measurement of the spectrometer. For the mSMUI of the WDM-system, no MUI occurs and is set to zero. The noise consists of its mean value $\overline{N}$ plus its standard deviation $\sigma(N)$ which leads to a result of

$$\mathrm{mSMUI_{WDM}} = \frac{59290\,\mathrm{Counts}}{3379\,\mathrm{Counts} + 10\,\mathrm{Counts}} = 17.49 \,\hat{=}\, 12.43\,\mathrm{dB}. \qquad (5)$$

This measurement shows that the CDM-system can be a reliable multiplexing technique besides WDM in terms of noise and signal quality.

6   Hybrid CDM-WDM

The results in the previous sections have shown, that this CDM approach is suitable to multiplex FBG sensors. On the other hand, WDM is a well established

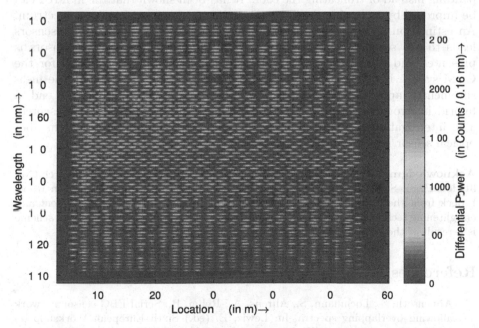

Fig. 11. Interrogation of 2000 serial FBG sensors in hybrid CDM-WDM multiplex network [9].

interrogation scheme in FBG sensor networks. A combination of CDM and WDM leads to a hybrid multiplexing scheme. The amount of WDM multiplexed sensors in a network can be multiplied by the amount of sensors operating at the same wavelength. The proof of concept is presented in detail in [9]. Due to the shape of the broadband light source, the peaks in the difference spectrum cannot use the complete capacity. It can be considered with the parameter ϵ in Fig. 9 and results in lower peaks for low and high wavelengths. The plot in Fig. 11 is realized by changing the synchronization delay nanosecond by nanosecond. The network consists of 25 WDM sections each containing 80 FBG at different wavelengths. The sensor network comprises an optical fiber with a 2.5 cm distance between each sensor. The total length results in ~50 m. Sensors at the same wavelength are 2 m apart so that a chip duration of 10 ns is used. This measurement in combination with the estimated limit shows a great potential in the field of massive serial fiber optical sensor networks.

7 Conclusion

This contribution analyzes the capability of a CDM interrogation scheme for serial FBGs with overlapping spectra. Different trigger schemes have been evaluated according to a modified signal to MUI ratio mSMUI. This modified parameter is suitable for CDM systems as well as WDM systems. The best scheme is to realize the code delay by using a rotated version of the code and a zero padding instead of truncating the code. It has been shown that the mSMUI can be improved by increasing the integration time for an acquisition of a spectrum. An estimation of the limit in terms of number of spectral overlapping sensors leads to 376 sensors. A measurement with 25 spectral overlapping sensors is presented and compared to a WDM system. Due to SIK the mSMUI for the CDM system is better than for a WDM system. The peak height in the measurement is approximately 70% of the theoretical peak height. At the end, a hybrid interrogation scheme, a combination of CDM and WDM is presented. The interrogation of 2000 sensors shows the great potential of CDM in fiber optical sensor networks.

Acknowledgment. Funded by the German Ministry of Education and Research (No. 3FH030PX8). Special thanks go to Eric Lindner, Johan Vlekken and Jan Van Roosbroeck from the company FBGS for their great support in terms of equipment and enlightening technical discussions. Especially the proposed hybrid interrogation scheme is a result of the great collaborational project work.

References

1. Abbenseth, S., Lochmann, S., Ahrens, A., Rehm, B.: Serial FBG sensor network allowing overlapping spectra. In: Lewis, E. (ed.) Sixth European Workshop on Optical Fibre Sensors. SPIE, May 2016. https://doi.org/10.1117/12.2235279

2. Abbenseth, S., Lochmann, S.I.: Distinct enlargement of network size or measurement speed for serial FBG sensor networks utilizing SIK-DS-CDMA. J. Phys: Conf. Ser. **15**, 149–154 (2005). https://doi.org/10.1088/1742-6596/15/1/025
3. Alwis, L., et al.: Integrated fiber Bragg grating incorporated textile carbon reinforcement structures. In: 2017 IEEE SENSORS. IEEE, October 2017. https://doi.org/10.1109/icsens.2017.8234106
4. Cano, W.F.R., et al.: Evaluation of FBG sensors to measure ultrasonic guided waves in rail transport monitoring. In: 2017 SBMO/IEEE MTT-S International Microwave and Optoelectronics Conference (IMOC). IEEE, August 2017. https://doi.org/10.1109/imoc.2017.8121167
5. Chang, C.H., Tsai, C.H.: A Large-Scale Optical Fiber Sensor Network With Reconfigurable Routing Path Functionality. IEEE Photonics J. **11**(3), 1–11 (2019). https://doi.org/10.1109/jphot.2019.2919196
6. Childers, B.A., et al.: Use of 3000 Bragg grating strain sensors distributed on four 8-m optical fibers during static load tests of a composite structure. In: McGowan, A.M.R. (ed.) Smart Structures and Materials 2001: Industrial and Commercial Applications of Smart Structures Technologies. SPIE, June 2001. https://doi.org/10.1117/12.429650
7. Chung, W., Tam, H.Y., Wai, P., Khandelwal, A.: Time- and wavelength-division multiplexing of FBG sensors using a semiconductor optical amplifier in ring cavity configuration. IEEE Photonics Technol. Lett. **17**(12), 2709–2711 (2005). https://doi.org/10.1109/lpt.2005.859484
8. Götten, M., Lochmann, S., Ahrens, A.: Analysis of non-ideal optical correlation for interrogating overlapping FBG spectra. In: 2018 Advances in Wireless and Optical Communications (RTUWO), pp. 154–160. IEEE, November 2018. https://doi.org/10.1109/rtuwo.2018.8587865
9. Götten, M., Lochmann, S., Ahrens, A., Lindner, E., Roosbroeck, J.V.: 2000 Serial FBG Sensors Interrogated With a Hybrid CDM-WDM Scheme. J. Lightwave Technol. **38**(8), 2493–2503 (2020). https://doi.org/10.1109/jlt.2020.2974344
10. Götten, M., Lochmann, S., Ahrens, A., Benavente-Peces, C.: A robust serial FBG sensor network with CDM interrogation allowing overlapping spectra. In: Proceedings of the 9th International Conference on Sensor Networks. SCITEPRESS - Science and Technology Publications (2020). https://doi.org/10.5220/0008942900230028
11. smail, M., et al.: Fiber Bragg grating-based Fabry-Perot interferometer sensor for damage detection on thin aluminum plate. IEEE Sens. J. **20**(7), 3564–3571 (2020). https://doi.org/10.1109/jsen.2019.2959068
12. Jelbuldina, M., Korobeinyk, A., Korganbayev, S., Tosi, D., Dukenbayev, K., Inglezakis, V.J.: Real-time temperature monitoring in liver during magnetite nanoparticle-enhanced microwave ablation with fiber Bragg grating sensors: ex vivo analysis. IEEE Sens. J. **18**(19), 8005–8011 (2018). https://doi.org/10.1109/jsen.2018.2865100
13. Kaplan, N., Jasenek, J., Cervenova, J., Usakova, M.: Magnetic optical FBG sensors using optical frequency-domain reflectometry. IEEE Trans. Magn. **55**(1), 1–4 (2019). https://doi.org/10.1109/tmag.2018.2873405
14. Middlestead, R.W.: Spread-Spectrum Communications, pp. 485–529. John Wiley & Sons, Inc., March 2017. https://doi.org/10.1002/9781119011866.ch13
15. O'Farrell, T., Lochmann, S.: Performance analysis of an optical correlator receiver for SIK DS-CDMA communication systems. Electron. Lett. **30**(1), 63–65 (1994). https://doi.org/10.1049/el:19940069

16. Ou, Y., et al.: Large WDM FBG sensor network based on frequency-shifted inter-
    ferometry. IEEE Photonics Technol. Lett. **29**(6), 535–538 (2017). https://doi.org/
    10.1109/lpt.2017.2663665
17. Presti, D.L., et al.: Wearable system based on flexible FBG for respiratory and
    cardiac monitoring. IEEE Sens. J. **19**(17), 7391–7398 (2019). https://doi.org/10.
    1109/jsen.2019.2916320
18. Rajan, G. (Ed.): Optical Fiber Sensors: Advanced Techniques and Appli-
    cations. CRC Press Inc. (2015), https://www.ebook.de/de/product/23194884/
    optical_fiber_sensors_advanced_techniques_and_applications.html
19. Senkans, U., et al.: FBG sensors network embedded in spectrum-sliced WDM-PON
    transmission system operating on single shared broadband light source. In: 2019
    Photonics & Electromagnetics Research Symposium - Fall (PIERS - Fall). IEEE,
    December 2019. https://doi.org/10.1109/piers-fall48861.2019.9021628
20. Song, Y., Xia, L., Wu, Y.: The interrogation of quasi-distributed optical FBG sens-
    ing system through adopting a wavelength-tunable fiber chaotic laser. J. Lightwave
    Technol. **37**(10), 2435–2442 (2019). https://doi.org/10.1109/jlt.2019.2907278
21. Tosi, D.: Review and analysis of peak tracking techniques for fiber bragg grating
    sensors. Sensors **17**(10), 2368 (2017). https://doi.org/10.3390/s17102368
22. Triana, A., Pastor, D., Varón, M.: Code division multiplexing applied to FBG
    sensing networks: FBG sensors designed as discrete prolate spheroidal sequences
    (DPSS-FBG Sensors). J. Lightwave Technol. **35**(14), 2880–2886, July 2017.
    https://doi.org/10.1109/jlt.2017.2705283
23. Wang, Y., Gong, J., Dong, B., Wang, D.Y., Shillig, T.J., Wang, A.: A large serial
    time-division multiplexed fiber Bragg grating sensor network. J. Lightwave Tech-
    nol. **30**(17), 2751–2756 (2012). https://doi.org/10.1109/jlt.2012.2205897

Strength Exercise Monitoring with Inertial Sensors

Sarvenaz Salehi[1(✉)] and Didier Stricker[2]

[1] Daimler Protics, Leinfelden-Echterdingen, Germany
Sarvenaz.Salehi_Mourkani@daimler.com
[2] German Research Center for Artificial Intelligence (DFKI),
Kaiserslautern, Germany
Didier.Stricker@dfki.de

Abstract. To monitor the strength exercises, the idea is to capture a template signal while instructing users to perform the movements correctly according to their ability and state of health. This template is used in an online template-matching algorithm based on DTW that was evaluated using the join angles and segment positions estimated by the pose estimation approach, while users performed the squat exercise. This method is optimized using a motion primitive detection technique and feature extraction. The results show that compared to other optimization approaches, the proposed method led to a lower execution time while maintaining a good accuracy. This effectively provides a measure for RM, which is one of the critical factors in monitoring strength exercises.

Keywords: Inertial sensors · Motion tracking · Online template matching · Dynamic time warping · Strength exercise monitoring

1 Introduction

Strength is the ability of a muscle or a group of muscles with the same functional role in producing force, which is critical for athletic performance, as well as for activities of daily living [9]. The assessment of this quantity helps physicians and therapists plan programs to maintain and develop strength [4]. The benefits of monitoring strength exercise in terms of performance improvement, injury prevention, and rehabilitation are discussed in various studies [10,21]. Performance improvement is achieved by monitoring the strength exercises by measuring Repetition Maximum (RM) [13], which can be achieved by consistently indicating the number of repetitions during the exercise. Therefore, a system is needed that tracks the movements precisely and recognizes the correctly performed exercises [17,18]. The exercise identification process, which is based on a precise tracking of lower body movements, provides the repetition numbers that can later be used to evaluate user performance in relation to RM. Moreover, external motivation to improve the performance can be achieved by receiving visual feedback from the monitoring system of the identified phases of the exercise.

By consistently estimating the joint angles of the lower extremities, such a system provides a reliable measure of Range of Motion (RoM) [16,19], which is the most important factor in the detection and prevention of injuries [8]. Furthermore, the quantification

© Springer Nature Switzerland AG 2022
A. Ahrens et al. (Eds.): SENSORNETS 2020/2021, CCIS 1674, pp. 39–59, 2022.
https://doi.org/10.1007/978-3-031-17718-7_3

of the imbalances can be achieved by such a platform, which additionally provides a precise estimation of the leg segment positions. The knee joint angle is used to identify each stage of the rehabilitation process. Moreover, the symmetrical execution of the strength exercise can be recognized as a factor in the progress of rehabilitation by tracking the leg segment positions. In addition to the knee joint angle, the 3D estimation of the hip joint angle helps to control the dynamics by detecting abduction and internal rotation during flexion.

In rehabilitation clinics, these values are usually measured manually using goniometers. However, this procedure is time-consuming and cumbersome and cannot provide precise measurements in dynamic situations [12]. Moreover, clinicians need to be trained in the correct placement of such devices, and therefore it is imperative that patients go to rehabilitation centers to monitor their progress in recovery. In our previous work [19] we proposed the process of Body-IMU calibration and lower body pose estimation and identification including experimental results. In this work we explain the identification method in more details and extended evaluation. The focus is on online template matching approaches based on Dynamic Time Warping (DTW). Section 2 addresses the related work and challenges of DTW-based approaches and describes four various methods in the related work for optimizing their performance. Section 3 presents the proposed method. Section 4 evaluates and compares the result of the formerly discussed methods, in the application of squat exercise identification using two different types of motion signals and in terms of accuracy and execution time.

2 Related Work

The DTW transformation [1] calculates minimum distances between the two signal sequences, regardless of the difference in acceleration and deceleration. This means, this algorithm uses an elastic transformation of the time series to recognize similar shapes with different phases. If $X = (x_1, ..., x_n)$ is the source sequence and $Y = (y_1, ..., y_m)$ is the query sequence and $X, Y \in \Phi$, where Φ is the feature space, the DTW transformation is $d : \Phi \times \Phi \to \mathbb{R} \geq 0$. The algorithm first builds up a local cost matrix C_l, which contains all the pairwise distances between the features in X and Y as follows:

$$C_l \in \mathbb{R}^{n \times m}, c_{i,j} = \| c_i - c_j \|, i \in 1, ..., n, j \in 1, ..., m, \tag{1}$$

where $\| . \|$ is the vector norm. The areas of the matrix with the minimum values define the warping path.

This method has a time complexity of $O(n^2)$. Therefore, it is efficient for a finite number of features in X. With increasing length of X, for example, in the case of a real time exercise identification process with a stream of features, the number of possible warping paths grows exponentially. Therefore, a dynamic programming approach is introduced to reduce complexity as follows:

$$dtw(i, j) = c_{i,j} + min \begin{cases} dtw(i, j - 1) \\ dtw(i - 1, j) \\ dtw(i - 1, j - 1) \end{cases}$$
$$dtw(0, 0) = 0, dtw(i, 0) = dtw(0, j) = \infty \tag{2}$$
$$(i = 1, ..., n; j = 1, ..., m),$$

where $c_{i,j}$ is defined in (1). This reduces the temporal and spatial complexity to $O(mn)$, which is still not applicable for online template matching of streaming data. There are many different proposed methods for accelerating the DTW, such as lower bounding in [6], where the range of the search for the warping path is limited, or the early abandoning in [7] that consists of starting an incremental computation of DTW and stopping if it exceeds a lower bound. However, these methods can not solve the problem of template matching for online streaming. Rkthanmanon et al. in [14] propose UCR-DTW, combining eight techniques to accelerate DTW. The experimental results show that this method has a low computational time and high accuracy. However, it is assumed that the subsequence and query have the same length. Moreover, the combination of several techniques results in a complex structure. In [15] Sakurai et al. have introduced an efficient DTW-based method with a simple structure for monitoring the streaming subsequences, which reduces the temporal and spatial complexity to $O(n)$. This approach is discussed in detail in the next Section.

Other than accelerating and improving the storage requirement, there are some proposed methods to increase the accuracy while maintaining the time complexity, mostly based on the normalization idea; As described in [14] in the problem of identification of video images, the scale can change due to many factors, such as camera zooming, camera tilt angle, or for example, different clothing of the subject. Therefore, they should be normalized for a meaningful calculation of distances between the template and the video sequences. In the normalization process, the query and streaming subsequence are transformed into comparable ranges. Therefore, the different amplitude levels can not be mistaken with different structures. [3, 14] propose z-score normalization during online streaming based on SPRING using a fixed-length sliding window. As different sizes of the window can cause unwanted fluctuations, which affect the robustness of DTW against disturbances in the time axis, [23] proposes a dynamic z-score normalization. To solve the problem of z-score normalization, where z-score coefficient changes frequently in a data stream, [2] proposes an online min-max normalization for improving SPRING. However, none of these works directly considers higher data dimensions, which can highly degrade the optimization of accuracy and speed for online DTW-based approaches. In the current work, the proposed solutions in [2, 3], and [23] are discussed and evaluated for exercise identification with one-dimensional data from the knee joint angle. In addition, [3] and [23] are extended to consider higher data dimensions, as it is critical for such application.

Approximation based approaches, such as Piecewise Aggregated Approximation (PAA) [5], attempt to reduce the processing time by transforming the original sequence into a symbolic representation. In PAA, the equal-lengthed intervals of a sequence are approximated by their mean values. Based on PAA, iSax technique, one of the most powerful indexing techniques, was developed in [20] using Euclidean distances. It is shown that iSax is very accurate and fast. However, using Euclidean distance as the similarity measure makes it vulnerable in dealing with the time fluctuations. In this work, the concept of PAA is adopted and extended to other features besides mean value, in order to increase the efficiency of the online DTW-based approach in SPRING [15].

2.1 SPRING

SPRING introduces a new definition of the distance matrix, known as subsequence time warping matrix (STWM), where each cell contains $d(t, i)$, which is the best distance to match $X[t]$ to $Y[i]$, along with the start position $s(t, i)$. In other words, the $d(t, i)$ is the distance of a subsequence starting from $s(t, i)$ to t. This leads to a reduction in the processing time and space required to store DTW matrix. In fact, only two arrays of length of the query, m, related to the distances and start points, should be stored and updated at every each sample arrival.

The distance in SPRING is calculated as follows:

$$d(t, i) = \| x_t - y_i \| + d_{best},$$

$$d_{best} = min \begin{cases} d(t, i - 1) \\ d(t - 1, i) \\ d(t - 1, i - 1) \end{cases}$$

$$d(t, 0) = 0, d(0, i) = \infty$$

$$(t = 1, ..., n; i = 1, ..., m).$$

(3)

Therefore, the starting points should be updated according to the new distance in Eq. (4):

$$s(t, i) = \begin{cases} s(t, i - 1) & (d(t, i - 1) = d_{best}) \\ s(t - 1, i) & (d(t, i - 1) = d_{best}) \\ s(t - 1, i - 1) & (d(t - 1, i - 1) = d_{best}) \end{cases}$$

(4)

There are two different types of subsequent matching: best query and range query. While range query finds a local minimum, the best query, among all the possible subsequences, finds a subsequent with the shortest distance from a query Y starting at each sample received, $X[t_s]$.

For online streaming data with semi-infinite length, the range query is preferable to the best query. To avoid the heavily overlapping matched subsequences, SPRING proposes a modified range query called disjoint query with an additional condition such that among all the subsequences close enough to the query sequence, $dtw(X[t_s : t_e], Y) < \epsilon_0$, the algorithm reports only the local minimum; which means the distance is the smallest.

Therefore, after the operation in Eq. 4 start and end time of a best-so-far found subsequence and its DTW distance to the query are updated respectively: $t_s = s(t, m)$, $t_e = t$, and $d_{min} = d(t, m)$, when condition $d(t, m) < d_{min} \wedge d(t, m) \le \epsilon$ is true.

According to disjoint query, the matched subsequence at time $t - 1$ is reported at time t if none of the updated entries of $d(t, k)$ with $k = 1, .., m$ follows the previous condition, unless its start time is after previously detected end time, in that case, it possibly belongs to the next matching subsequence. The condition for reporting the matched subsequence can be summarized as:

$$d_{min} \le \epsilon \wedge (\forall d(t, k) > d_{min} \vee s(t, m) > t_e)$$

(5)

Before the next search starts, d_{min} and all the entries of the list d whose starting time are before t_e are set to infinity, so that a currently matched subsequence is not considered in the next search. At the end of each time point, the old lists are substituted by the new lists. At each time tick only two lists of size m have to be updated and only four lists need to be stored. SPRING has a simple structure and can be implemented with few lines of code. Moreover, query and subsequence from stream don't need to have a similar length, as is required for UCR-DTW [14]. In addition, this approach can be easily extended to multidimensional queries and subsequences. However, this increases the execution time, as shown in the experimental results in Sect. 4.

3 Proposed Method

In this work on the basis of SPRING a method is proposed to increase the temporal and spatial efficiency, while maintaining the accuracy, specifically for the application of exercise identification. As discussed in the previous sections, the proposed optimizations of online DTW-based approaches lack the consideration for multidimensional input data. This impedes applying such methods for strength exercise monitoring, where the motion signals, including multiple DOFs, define a correctly performed exercise. Therefore, the proposed method optimizes SPRING to support multidimensional data by exploiting the common characteristics of the motion signals based on two concepts of motion primitive detection and feature extraction. These concepts and the procedure of identification are explained in the following sections.

3.1 Motion Primitive Detection

Since a strength exercise usually contains a periodic pattern in which the velocity of movement increases and decreases sequentially, the Zero Velocity Crossing (ZVC) method is chosen to detect the motion primitives in both query and streaming signal. Therefore, a motion primitive is detected, where the sign of derivative is changing on the dominant DOF of motion signals, e.g. positions or joint angles. The derivative is calculated here, with a numerical differentiation over a sliding window. This causes a delay in reporting the identified movements i.e. half of the window length. However, to detect the motion primitives where the velocity changes abruptly, this window length needs to be small. Consequently, the delay is small as well. The dominant DOF is selected on each dataset by finding a dimension of the query signal, which has the highest standard deviation and thus the greatest variations. The detected motion primitives in a query of joint angles are presented in Fig. 1, where the knee joint angle is a dominant DOF.

3.2 Feature Extraction

The features including velocity, variance, and mean value are selected in this approach, Fig. 1, as they define the movements by introducing the higher level information from the original motion signals. These features are calculated from each DOF of motion primitive. Therefore, for each motion primitive, tens of position or joint angle samples, as the input to the online identification algorithm, are reduced to three features in each dimension. This, as shown in the experimental results, has highly increased the speed of the identification algorithm while maintaining its accuracy.

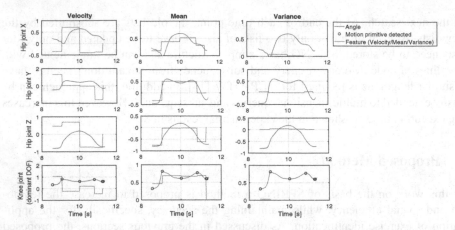

Fig. 1. Feature extraction of query signal using the proposed method. The query contains 4DOF joint angles captured during a squat exercise. Each DOF is defined by three different features: velocity, mean, and variance. These are correlated with each detected motion primitive. The detection motion primitives are presented by the black circle markers on the knee joint angle, as it has the highest variance and serves as a dominant DOF.

3.3 Identification

The proposed identification method is described in Algorithm 1. Using the approach described in Sect. 3.1, the dominant DOF is determined from the query. This is used in the ZVC method to detect the motion primitives associated with each DOF (see Algorithm 2), both in the query and in the streaming motion signal. The features, including mean and variance are calculated incrementally and extracted after a motion primitive is detected. For velocity the incremental calculation is not applied, as the higher number of points involved in the numerical differentiation leads to less error [11]. For each motion primitive, all types of features from all DOFs generate a feature vector. This is achieved by Algorithms 3 and 4. The latter explains the velocity calculation in which one of the three different numerical differentiation techniques, i.e. five-point stencil, symmetric and Newton's quotient [11], are applied depending on number of sample points available. This number in the motion primitive detection is equal to the half of the length of sliding window and in the feature extraction is equal to the number of samples in each motion primitive. The feature vectors together with the timestamps of their associated motion primitives are used to calculate the distance required for DTW in SPRING approach (Sect. 2.1); In Eq. 3, y_i and x_t can each be replaced by the feature vector of the motion primitive i in the query signal and of the motion primitive t in the streaming signal.

4   Experimental Results

Five online template matching methods described before, are implemented and evaluated in Matlab to identify the strength exercise of squat in a stream of motion signal. The input data is the result of lower body estimated pose using the approach explained

---

Algorithm 1. Proposed Exercise Identifier.

Initialization:
determine the dominant degree of freedom, DOF_d
set len to half of the length of sliding window rounded up, i.e. $ceiling(WinLength/2)$
Input: a new value of x_t
Output: start and stop points of a matched subsequence if any
1: $sum1 = sum1 + x_t$;
2: $sum2 = sum2 + x_t^2$;
3: Insert $sum1$ in $S1$;
4: Insert $sum2$ in $S2$;
5: Insert x_t in S;
6: Insert t in T;
7: $ls = length(S)$;
8: **if** $ls > len$ **then**
9:     $v_t = CalculateVelocity(S(ls - len : ls, DOF_d), T(ls - len : ls, DOF_d))$;
10:     Insert v_t into V;
11: **end if**
12: **if** $length(V) == len + 1$ **then**
13:     **if** $MotionPrimitiveDetected(V(1), V(len + 1))$ **then**
14:         $CurrentSpringTime = T(ls - len)$;
15:         $f = FeatureExtraction(S, T, S1(ls - len), S2(ls - len), ls - len)$;
16:         $[F_{Matched}, t_{start}, t_{stop}, d_{min}] = SPRING(f, CurrentSpringTime, t_{start},$
        $t_{stop}, d_{min})$;
17:         **if** $F_{Matched}$ **then**
18:             **return** $t_{start}, t_{stop}, d_{min}$;
19:         **end if**
20:         $S = S1(ls - len : ls)$;
21:         $S1 = S1(ls - len : ls) - S1(s - len - 1)$;
22:         $S2 = S2(ls - len : ls) - S2(s - len - 1)$;
23:         $sum1 = S1(len)$;
24:         $sum2 = S2(len)$;
25:         $V = V(len)$;
26:     **else**
27:         delete $V(1)$ from V;
28:     **end if**
29: **end if**

---

in [19], during an experiment with 7 subjects, in which they performed squat exercises together with other movements. In this experiment, the first squat, which was performed on the instruction of a supervisor, served as a template to identify the next repetitions in the streaming motion signal. After squats, the subjects performed other movements.

Streaming signals in all the test trials from all subjects contain some random movements and similar exercises such as squats, hip abduction/adductions, knee flexion/extensions, etc. The signal duration is, on average, 1 min, which means receiving around 6000 samples.

The execution time of each method is measured using TIC function in Matlab, which includes the processing time of query normalization and feature extraction in

---

Algorithm 2. Motion Primitive Detected.

Input: $V_{prev}, V_{current}(\epsilon = 1e^{-5})$

Output: True if it is detected and False otherwise.

    return $(V_{prev} <= \epsilon$ **and** $V_{current} >= \epsilon)$or$(V_{prev} >= \epsilon$ **and** $V_{current} <= \epsilon)$;

Algorithm 3. Feature Extraction.

Input: $S, T, S1, S2, len_{average}$

Output: feature vector

1: $f(1 : DataDimension) = calculateVelocity(S, T)$;
2: $Mean = S1/len_{average}$;
3: $f(DataDimension + 1 : 2 * DataDimension) = Mean$;
4: $f(2 * DataDimension + 1 : 3 * DataDimension) = S2/len_{average} - Mean^2$;
5: **return** f;

Algorithm 4. Calculate Velocity.

Input: S, T

Output: Average velocity of S.

1: $ls = length(S)$;
2: **for** $i \leftarrow 1$ to $DataDimension$ **do**
3:    $v(i) = 0, counter = 0$;
4:    **if** $ls \geq 5$ **then**
5:       **for** $j \leftarrow 3$ to $ls - 2$ **do**
6:          $h = T(j) - T(j - 1)$
7:          //five-point stencil
8:          $v(i) = v(i) + (S(j - 2, i) - 8 * S(j - 1, i) + 8 * S(j + 1, i) - S(j + 2, i))/(12 * h)$;
9:          $counter = counter + 1$;
10:       **end for**
11:    **else if** $ls \geq 3$ **then**
12:       //symmetric difference quotient
13:       **for** $j \leftarrow 2$ to $ls - 1$ **do**
14:          $h = T(j) - T(j - 1)$
15:          $v(i) = v(i) + (S(j + 1, i) - S(j - 1, i))/(2 * h)$;
16:          $counter = counter + 1$;
17:       **end for**
18:    **else if** $ls == 2$ **then**
19:       //Newton's difference quotient
20:       $h = T(2) - T(1)$
21:       $v(i) = (S(2, i) - S(1, i))/h$;
22:       $counter = 1$;
23:    **end if**
24:    $v(i) = v(i)/counter$;
25: **end for**
26: **return** v

addition to stream data identification. For the proposed method the time to detect the dominant DOF is also considered in execution time.

The common performance metrics, accuracy, precision, recall, and $F1$ score are measured based on the comparison of algorithmic and manual identification. This comparison provides the number of true positives (TP), false positives (FP), true negatives (TN), and false negatives (FN) out of the total number of features in the streaming signal. These are used in the following formulas in order to calculate those metrics:

$$Accuracy = \frac{TP + TN}{total} \tag{6a}$$

$$Precision = \frac{TP}{TP + FP} \tag{6b}$$

$$Recall = \frac{TP}{TP + FN} \tag{6c}$$

$$F1score = \frac{2 \times Recall \times Precision}{Recall + Precision} \tag{6d}$$

For a fair comparative evaluation, all the methods which include the disjoint query are tuned for the threshold ϵ in the inequality of (5) and separately for each type of movement, so that they identify at least one TP in three of the trials. The tuning starts with a value in the range of the distances in the middle of STWM column and increasing it till a TP is found. The following sections present the evaluation of the results of each method.

4.1 Identification with SPRING

SPRING method is implemented here as proposed in [15]. Therefore, no feature extraction is required. However, to have the same range in all DOFs, each vector sample of joint angles, including hip and knee joint, is normalized.

The method is used for squat exercise identification with three different types of motion signals: 1DOF: only knee joint angle, 4 DOF: hip and knee joint angles, 6DOF: upper and lower leg segment positions. Results in terms of performance metrics and execution time are presented in Tables 1, 2, and 3. The best performance is related to test with the position signals as the squat can be identified better, among other movements, by incorporating more DOFs. As expected, the execution time for processing 1DOF is less than the other tests.

For a detailed analysis of the process of online DTW, embedded in SPRING method, the STWM matrix is visualized in Fig. 2, where the darker colour indicates lower values, and the lighter colour higher values. This is collected from the test with 4DOF joint angles. It can be easily noticed there's a high amount of data, which should be processed at each sample arrival in order to update all the values in a related column. This is one of the disadvantages of SPRING which leads to high execution time especially when the query is large. Moreover, in this example the algorithm fails to identify the forth and seventh performed squats. This can be due to a slight difference in the amplitude of the second DOF, hip_Y, at the end of the movement, where it has a delay to rise from its minimum compared to other DOFs. This is visible in Fig. 2, where the STWM column after the identified subsequence is only light in the middle and not in the lower area, where the distances to the end of query exist. This as well delays reporting the identification due to disjoint query as the algorithm searches for a better transition in the shape of the signal. As the experiment with the proposed method in Sect. 4.5 shows, such amplitude deficiencies do not influence the result as other high level features are involved in the identification process.

Table 1. Squat identification with knee joint angle based on SPRING method.

	Squat						
	subj. 1	subj. 2	subj. 3	subj. 4	subj. 5	subj. 6	subj. 7
Accuracy [%]	99.9	99.9	99.9	99.8	99.9	99.8	99.5
Precision [%]	50.0	50.0	71.4	40.0	60.0	40.0	16.0
Recall [%]	50.0	40.0	100.0	80.0	85.7	80.0	80.0
F1 score [%]	50.0	44.4	83.3	53.3	70.6	53.3	26.6
Execution time [s]	3.16	1.98	1.76	1.16	1.60	2.80	1.42

Table 2. Squat identification with knee and hip joint angles based on SPRING method.

	SPRING						
	subj. 1	subj. 2	subj. 3	subj. 4	subj. 5	subj. 6	subj. 7
Accuracy [%]	99.4	99.7	99.4	99.8	99.6	99.9	99.9
Precision [%]	100.0	31.2	100.0	40.0	100.0	100.0	83.3
Recall [%]	25.0	100.0	40.0	80.0	71.0	40.0	100.0
F1 score [%]	40.0	47.6	57.1	53.3	83.3	57.1	90.9
Execution time [s]	3.22	2.58	2.29	1.43	2.08	3.56	1.77

Table 3. Squat identification with leg positions based on SPRING method.

	SPRING						
	subj. 1	subj. 2	subj. 3	subj. 4	subj. 5	subj. 6	subj. 7
Accuracy [%]	99.9	99.9	99.9	99.9	99.9	99.9	99.9
Precision [%]	100.0	100.0	100.0	100.0	100.0	100.0	83.3
Recall [%]	50.0	80.0	60.0	60.0	42.8	20.0	100.0
F1 score [%]	66.6	88.8	75.0	75.0	60.0	33.3	90.9
Execution time [s]	2.97	1.90	2.08	1.45	2.31	3.71	1.44

4.2 Identification with ISPRING

As the search for min-max coefficients in each DOF, which is required for normalization in ISPRING method, affects the warping distance calculations, it is not practical

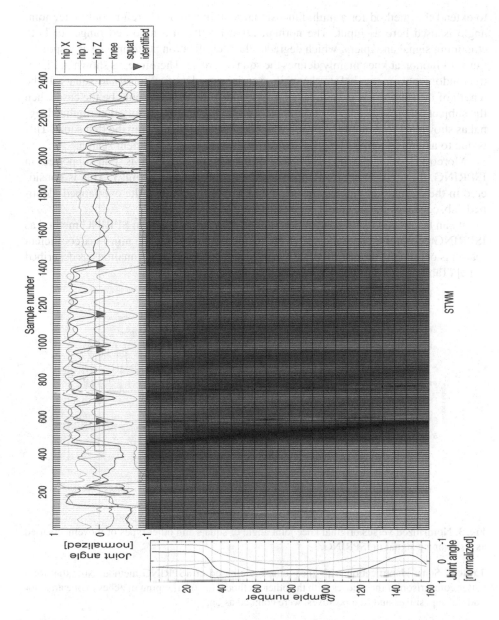

Fig. 2. The STWM matrix in SPRING for an experiment with 4DOF joint angles: The values of this matrix, dtw distances, are normalized by the maximum value and presented by a built-in Colormap in Matlab, where darker colours depict the lower values. Therefore, the warping path of a matched subsequence can be identified, where there is a continuous darker area from the first to the last row. For brevity, this matrix is scaled down 10 and 5 times along the row and column. The streaming signal and the query are represented at the top and left side. Note that each joint angle vector is normalized.

to extend this method for a multidimensional identification. Therefore only knee joint angle is used here as input. The normalization results in a modified range for both streaming signal and query, which degrades the identification performance as a specific range of motion at knee mainly defines the squat exercise. Therefore, as shown in Fig. 3, the random movements before the main exercise are identified falsely as squats. If the length of the subsequence candidate is less than the query, as it could be the case when the subject performs squats with different speeds, it leads to a distorted normalized signal as shown in the example of Fig. 3, which leads to fail identifying the first squat. This is due to assuming a fixed-length window for the min-max coefficient search.

Moreover, since the disjoint query proposed in SPRING is not supported in ISPRING, there are many overlapped matching subsequences, Fig. 3. This is considered in the calculation of performance metrics by discarding all the overlapped identified subsequences in one area.

It can be noticed that the execution time in all trials is less than SPRING method as ISPRING does not include the search for disjoint query. Also, the min-max coefficient search is optimal by deploying Binary search and Quicksort functionalities as described in [2] (Table 4).

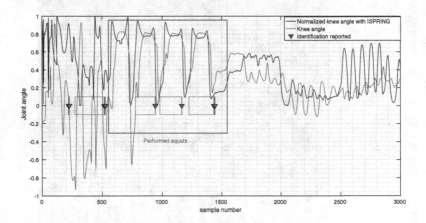

Fig. 3. Normalized versus original knee joint angle of squats and other types of movements used as a streaming signal in ISPRING.

Table 4. Squat identification with knee joint angle based on ISPRING method. Note that for a better comparison of the metrics with the other methods, the overlapping matches in one area, for both false positives and true positives, were counted as one.

	Squat						
	subj. 1	subj. 2	subj. 3	subj. 4	subj. 5	subj. 6	subj. 7
Accuracy [%]	92.5	95.32	91.52	92.63	78.94	96.47	50
Precision [%]	60.0	50.0	50.0	25.0	0	75.0	0
Recall [%]	75.0	20.0	20.0	20.0	0	60	0
F1 score [%]	66.66	28.57	28.57	22.22	0	66.66	0
Execution time [s]	2.32	1.58	1.14	0.71	2.19	1.14	1.07

4.3 Identification with NSPRING

The normalized signal according to NSPRING method is calculated using $\frac{x_{t'}-M(t',i)}{SD(t',i)}$.
In this experiment, the normalization results in the inconsistency, which is caused
by extremely small standard deviations and division by such values. This problem is
resolved to some extent by considering a lower bound of 10^{-6} and resetting to this value
when the standard deviation is lower. Note that in the test with 4DOF joint angles, these
values are not normalized as it caused similar numerical problems. Figure 4 shows this
problem, which causes the query and streaming signals to not always be in the same
range in contrast to what is expected from a normalization process. As a result, the
overall performance of this method is worse than SPRING while the execution time
is higher especially for 4DOF data, Table 6. This is due to four added lists of M and
SD for each DOF, which have to be maintained and/or updated at receiving each new
sample. Moreover, as described in [3], there is an inherit delay in reporting the identification, Fig. 4. The result here is not compatible with [3] since they claimed that they
achieve the same results as SPRING. However, they used different performance metrics
and input signals for their evaluations, which could justify this different outcome.

This method is evaluated for both one dimensional and multidimensional joint angle
signals, Tables 5, 6, as well as for multidimensional leg segment position signal. The
latter is not presented here, due to the poor performance of this algorithm, where the ϵ
threshold tuning process fails to achieve any true positives in any of the trials.

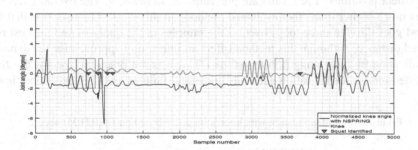

Fig. 4. Normalized versus original knee joint angle of squats and other types of movements used
as a streaming signal in NSPRING.

Table 5. Squat identification with knee joint angle based on NSPRING method.

	SPRING						
	subj. 1	subj. 2	subj. 3	subj. 4	subj. 5	subj. 6	subj. 7
Accuracy [%]	99.87	99.85	99.74	99.72	99.91	99.89	99.70
Precision [%]	25.0	0	0	16.67	80.0	0	9.09
Recall [%]	25.0	0	0	40.0	57.14	0	20.0
F1 score [%]	25.0	0	0	23.53	66.67	0	12.50
Execution time [s]	3.61	2.83	2.50	1.65	3.13	3.83	2.04

4.4   Identification with DNRTPM

The normalization process of DNRTPM is evaluated using the knee joint angle. The similar problem of numerical inconsistency in NSPRING is evident in the normalized signal by DNRTPM as they both apply z-score normalization, Fig. 5. However, the precision here is slightly better, see Table 7, as the z-score normalization is refined using amplification and offset correction proposed in [22].

Table 6. Squat identification with knee and hip joint angles based on NSPRING method.

	SPRING						
	subj. 1	subj. 2	subj. 3	subj. 4	subj. 5	subj. 6	subj. 7
Accuracy [%]	99.91	99.89	99.91	98.26	99.79	99.82	99.25
Precision [%]	0	0.5000	66.67	5.75	41.18	0	10.53
Recall [%]	0	20.0	40.0	100.0	100.0	0	80.0
F1 score [%]	0	28.57	50.0	10.87	58.33	0	18.60
Execution time [s]	7.90	6.23	5.30	4.01	5.10	8.40	4.32

This algorithm is further developed to be used for multidimensional joint angles and leg segment positions. The results are presented in Tables 8, 9. The overall execution time is much higher than other evaluated methods in this work. The reason is that this method goes through three loops over all the samples in the query to find the best normalized distance. Although this method offers an interesting approach for the dynamic normalization by integrating it in an online DTW, it is not practical, specifically for a real time exercise identification due to its numerical failures and high execution time.

Table 7. Squat identification with knee joint angle based on DNRTPM method.

	DNRTPM						
	subj. 1	subj. 2	subj. 3	subj. 4	subj. 5	subj. 6	subj. 7
Accuracy [%]	99.90	99.90	99.81	99.90	99.63	99.92	99.92
Precision [%]	33.33	0	16.67	0	26.09	100.0	100.0
Recall [%]	25.0	0	20.0	0	85.71	20.0	20.0
F1 Score [%]	28.57	0	18.18	0	40.0	33.33	33.33
Execution time [s]	26.65	21.48	19.32	13.89	19.46	32.95	16.64

Table 8. Squat identification with knee and hip joint angles based on DNRTPM method.

	DNRTPM						
	subj. 1	subj. 2	subj. 3	subj. 4	subj. 5	subj. 6	subj. 7
Accuracy [%]	99.92	99.90	99.77	99.44	99.85	99.90	99.77
Precision [%]	0	0	31.25	15.63	0	0	12.50
Recall [%]	0	0	100.0	100.0	0	0	20.0
F1 score [%]	0	0	47.62	27.03	0	0	15.38
Execution time [s]	35.71	29.24	24.75	16.21	23.25	41.04	19.98

Table 9. Squat identification with leg positions based on DNRTPM method.

	DNRTPM						
	subj. 1	subj. 2	subj. 3	subj. 4	subj. 5	subj. 6	subj. 7
Accuracy [%]	99.63	99.33	99.50	99.90	99.67	99.90	97.25
Precision [%]	6.25	9.09	17.24	0	23.53	0	3.65
Recall [%]	25.00	60.00	100.00	0	57.14	0	100.00
F1 score [%]	10.00	15.79	29.41	0	33.33	0	7.04
Execution time [s]	33.59	21.88	23.18	19.64	27.04	43.63	14.99

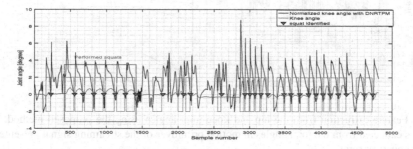

Fig. 5. Normalized versus original knee joint angle of squats and other types of movements used as a streaming signal in DNRTPM.

4.5 Identification with the Proposed Method

The proposed method, as described in Sect. 3 is developed and evaluated here for squat identification using different types of motion signals i.e. joint angles and leg segment positions. In this experiment, the length of sliding window is selected to be five as this reduces the velocity calculation for ZVC to one simple equation of symmetric quotient difference from three points, i.e. $ceiling(5/2)$.

The extracted features for both query and streaming signal are presented in Figs. 6 and 7. Each feature contains a higher level of information than the original signal, which further minimizes the DTW. This can be realized by comparing the features related to different movements in Figs. 6 and 7. Therefore, the identification performance is comparable with SPRING and higher than all the other methods as presented in Table 10, 11, 12. The exception here is the performance of SPRING method for position signals, which is higher than the proposed method. This can be due to minimal values of variance compared to other features. Further evaluation of different features and their effectiveness in the process of exercise identification is the subject of future work.

Each DOF adds three types of features. Therefore, for the case of 4DOF joint angles and 6DOF position signals the vector length is 12 and 18 respectively. The results in Tables 11 and 12 verify that this does not affect the execution time, as the proposed motion primitive detection technique in Sect. 3 reduces the number of times in which a column in STWM needs to be updated. As the length of query is reduced to its motion primitives, this results in further improvement of execution time as the number of distance calculations and the search path for disjoint query is shorter than the original signal.

Figure 8 provides a detailed analysis on how the STWM matrix is established in this method. In comparison to Fig. 2 for the same signal, this matrix has a smaller size,

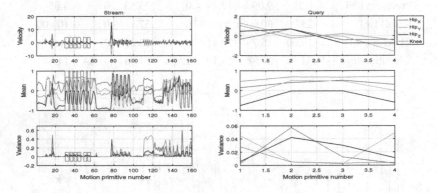

Fig. 6. Feature extraction from the hip and knee joint angles using the proposed method. The features extracted from the joint angles in motion primitives of the streaming signal presented at left and query at right.

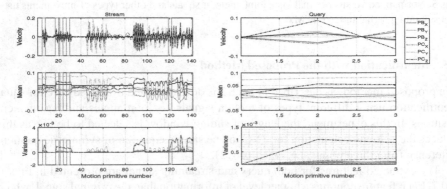

Fig. 7. Feature extraction from the leg positions using the proposed method. The features extracted from the leg segment positions in motion primitives of the streaming signal presented at left and query at right.

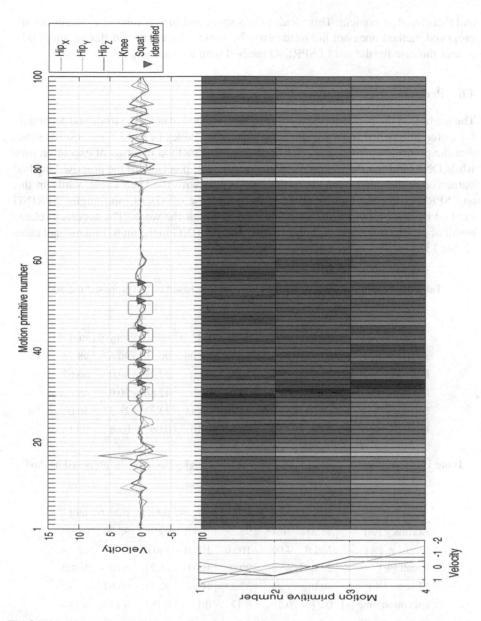

Fig. 8. The STWM matrix in the proposed method for an experiment with 4DOF joint angles: The values of this matrix, dtw distances, are normalized by the maximum value and presented by a built-in Colormap in Matlab, where darker colours depict the lower values. Therefore, the warping path of a matched subsequence can be identified, where there is a continuous darker area from the first to the last row. The number of rows and columns presented here correspond with the actual matrix, as a result of dimension reduction offered by the motion primitive technique in the proposed. The extracted features of streaming signal and the query are represented at the top and left side.

and therefore less content. This yields to less space and time complexity. Moreover, the proposed method does not fail to identify the subsequence with a different amplitude, as was the case for the test of SPRING method with the same signal.

4.6   Performance Comparison

The average of the performance metrics of each method over all the trials and separately for different types of input signals are presented in Tables 14 to 15. This result verifies that the proposed method outperforms all the other method in terms of execution time while DNRTPM has the worst time performance. The precision of the proposed method outperforms the other methods in the case of test with the knee angle, while in this test SPRING has the highest recall rate. In the case of 4DOF joint angles SPRING method has the best performance while DNRTPM has the worst. The accuracy related result of proposed method is slightly worse than SPRING in the multidimensional cases (Table 13).

Table 10. Squat identification with knee joint angle based on the proposed method.

	Proposed method						
	subj. 1	subj. 2	subj. 3	subj. 4	subj. 5	subj. 6	subj. 7
Accuracy [%]	97.92	97.52	97.58	96.09	90.16	96.67	98.37
Precision [%]	100.0	100.0	100.0	50.0	27.27	50.0	66.67
Recall [%]	25.00	20.0	20.0	40.0	42.86	20.0	40.0
F1 score [%]	40.00	33.33	33.33	44.44	33.33	28.57	50.0
Execution time [s]	0.24	0.11	0.11	0.10	0.09	0.08	0.11

Table 11. Squat identification with knee and hip joint angles based on the proposed method.

	Proposed method						
	subj. 1	subj. 2	subj. 3	subj. 4	subj. 5	subj. 6	subj. 7
Accuracy [%]	98.35	70.18	98.27	100.0	99.38	98.29	98.90
Precision [%]	100.0	4.00	100.0	100.0	100.0	75.0	62.50
Recall [%]	25.0	40.0	20.0	100.0	85.71	60.0	100.0
F1 score [%]	40.0	7.27	33.33	100.0	92.31	66.67	76.92
Execution time [s]	0.27	0.20	0.17	0.14	0.18	0.17	0.14

Table 12. Squat identification with leg positions based on the proposed method.

	Proposed method						
	subj. 1	subj. 2	subj. 3	subj. 4	subj. 5	subj. 6	subj. 7
Accuracy [%]	98.72	97.98	98.97	98.15	95.74	97.84	98.17
Precision [%]	100.0	100.0	100.0	100.0	60.0	100.0	66.67
Recall [%]	50.0	20.00	60.0	20.0	42.86	20.0	40.0
F1 score [%]	66.67	33.33	75.0	0.33	50.0	33.33	50.0
Execution time [s]	0.30	0.22	0.18	0.16	0.21	0.17	0.18

Table 13. Squat identification with the knee joint angle.

	Accuracy [%]	Precision [%]	Recall [%]	F1 Score [%]	Execution time [s]
SPRING	99.85	46.78	73.67	54.53	1.98
ISPRING	85.34	37.14	27.80	30.38	1.45
NSPRING	99.81	18.68	20.31	18.24	2.80
DNRTPM	99.85	39.44	24.39	21.92	21.49
Proposed method	96.33	70.56	29.69	37.57	0.12

Table 14. Squat identification with hip and knee joint angles.

	Accuracy [%]	Precision [%]	Recall [%]	F1 Score [%]	Execution time [s]
SPRING	99.91	79.23	65.20	61.35	2.42
NSPRING	99.55	24.88	48.57	23.77	5.90
DNRTPM	99.79	8.48	31.43	12.86	27.17
Proposed method	94.77	77.36	61.53	59.50	0.18

Table 15. Squat identification with leg positions.

	Accuracy [%]	Precision [%]	Recall [%]	F1 Score [%]	Execution time [s]
SPRING	99.95	97.62	58.98	69.97	2.26
DNRTPM	99.31	8.54	48.88	13.65	26.28
Proposed method	97.94	89.52	36.12	48.81	0.22

5   Conclusion

This work explains the application of online template matching for exercise identification, which provides real-time feedback to users by counting the number of correctly performed exercises. This can also be used to obtain a measure of repetition maximum (RM), which is one of the critical factors in monitoring the strength exercise. To optimize the procedure of online dynamic time warping approaches, a state of the art approach known as SPRING [15], and three modifications of it; ISPRING [2], NSPRING [3] and DNRTPM [23] are explained and analysed.

On the basis of SPRING, and inherit characteristics of motion signals, a new identification method is proposed. This method improves the temporal and spatial complexity of the online DTW-based approaches, by utilizing two concepts of motion primitive detection and feature extraction. Moreover, this method can be easily extended to support higher dimensions of input data, which makes it superior to the other optimization approaches, as they mainly rely on the normalization techniques with high complexities to increase the accuracy. These approaches are evaluated using different motion signals, i.e. hip and knee joint angles and the leg segments' positions for identification of the squat exercise in a streaming motion signal. The results show that the proposed method significantly improves the execution time while maintaining the accuracy. While this method outperforms other optimization approaches, it has comparable results and in some cases slightly worse performance than SPRING, in terms of precision and recall rate. This can be due to a low contribution of some features in the subsequence matching process, as observed for the case of variance feature in the experiments with the position signals. Since the proposed approach leads to high efficiency, the algorithm can be extended with additional features to further improve the accuracy without additional computational cost. Moreover, there are different exercise phases, e.g. concentric and eccentric phases of the squat, that could be identified differently depending on the characteristics or critical features for the correct performance.

References

1. Berndt, D.J., Clifford, J.: Using dynamic time warping to find patterns in time series. In: KDD Workshop, vol. 10, pp. 359–370. Seattle, WA (1994)
2. Giao, B.C., Anh, D.T.: Improving SPRING method in similarity search over time-series streams by data normalization. In: Vinh, P.C., Barolli, L. (eds.) ICTCC 2016. LNICST, vol. 168, pp. 189–202. Springer, Cham (2016). https://doi.org/10.1007/978-3-319-46909-6_18
3. Gong, X., Fong, S., Chan, J.H., Mohammed, S.: NSPRING: the spring extension for subsequence matching of time series supporting normalization. J. Supercomput. 72(10), 3801–3825 (2016)
4. Graves, J.E., et al.: Quantitative assessment of full range-of-motion isometric lumbar extension strength. Spine 15(4), 289–294 (1990)
5. Keogh, E., Chakrabarti, K., Pazzani, M., Mehrotra, S.: Dimensionality reduction for fast similarity search in large time series databases. Knowl. Inf. Syst. 3(3), 263–286 (2001)
6. Keogh, E., Ratanamahatana, C.A.: Exact indexing of dynamic time warping. Knowl. Inf. Syst. 7(3), 358–386 (2004). https://doi.org/10.1007/s10115-004-0154-9
7. Keogh, E., Wei, L., Xi, X., Vlachos, M., Lee, S.H., Protopapas, P.: Supporting exact indexing of arbitrarily rotated shapes and periodic time series under Euclidean and warping distance measures. VLDB J. 18(3), 611–630 (2009)
8. Kettunen, J.A., et al.: Factors associated with hip joint rotation in former elite athletes. Br. J. Sports Med. 34(1), 44–48 (2000)
9. Kulig, K., Andrews, J.G., Hay, J.G.: Human strength curves. Exerc. Sport Sci. Rev. 12(1), 417–466 (1984)
10. Mazzetti, S.A., et al.: The influence of direct supervision of resistance training on strength performance. Med. Sci. Sports Exerc. 32(6), 1175–1184 (2000)

11. Milne, W.E.: Numerical Solution of Differential Equations. Applied Mathematics Series. John Wiley & Sons, New York (1953)
12. van den Noort, J.C., Scholtes, V.A., Harlaar, J.: Evaluation of clinical spasticity assessment in cerebral palsy using inertial sensors. Gait Posture **30**(2), 138–143 (2009)
13. Powers, C.M.: The influence of abnormal hip mechanics on knee injury: a biomechanical perspective. J. Orthop. Sports Phys. Ther. **40**(2), 42–51 (2010)
14. Rakthanmanon, T., et al.: Searching and mining trillions of time series subsequences under dynamic time warping. In: Proceedings of the 18th ACM SIGKDD International Conference on Knowledge Discovery And Data Mining, pp. 262–270 (2012)
15. Sakurai, Y., Faloutsos, C., Yamamuro, M.: Stream monitoring under the time warping distance. In: 2007 IEEE 23rd International Conference on Data Engineering, pp. 1046–1055, April 2007. https://doi.org/10.1109/ICDE.2007.368963
16. Salehi, S., Bleser, G., Reiss, A., Stricker, D.: Body-IMU autocalibration for inertial hip and knee joint tracking. In: Proceedings of the 10th EAI International Conference on Body Area Networks, pp. 51–57. BodyNets 2015, ICST (Institute for Computer Sciences, Social-Informatics and Telecommunications Engineering), ICST, Brussels, Belgium, Belgium (2015). https://doi.org/10.4108/eai.28-9-2015.2261522
17. Salehi, S., Bleser, G., Schmitz, N., Stricker, D.: A low-cost and light-weight motion tracking suit. In: 10th International Conference on Ubiquitous Intelligence and Computing (UIC), pp. 474–479 (2013)
18. Salehi, S., Bleser, G., Stricker, D.: Design and development of low-cost smart training pants (STants). In: 4th International Conference on Wireless Mobile Communication and Healthcare, At Athen, Greece, pp. 39–44. IEEE (2014)
19. Salehi, S., Stricker, D.: Validation of a low-cost inertial exercise tracker. In: Prasad, C., Benavente-Peces, N. (Eds.) SENSORNETS 2021/SENSORNETS 2020, CCIS 1674, Proceedings of the 9th International Conference on Sensor Networks, pp. xx–yy. Sensornets (2020)
20. Shieh, J., Keogh, E.: iSAX: indexing and mining terabyte sized time series. In: Proceedings of the 14th ACM SIGKDD International Conference on Knowledge Discovery and Data Mining, pp. 623–631 (2008)
21. Snyder, K.R., Earl, J.E., O Connor, K.M., Ebersole, K.T.: Resistance training is accompanied by increases in hip strength and changes in lower extremity biomechanics during running. Clin. Biomech. **24**(1), 26–34 (2009)
22. Sukhanov, S., Wu, R., Debes, C., Zoubir, A.: Dynamic pattern matching with multiple queries on large scale data streams. Signal Process. **171**, 107402 (2020)
23. Wu, R., Sukhanov, S., Debes, C.: Real time pattern matching with dynamic normalization. arXiv preprint arXiv:1912.11977 (2019)

Improved Wake-Up Receiver Architectures with Carrier Sense Capabilities for Low-Power Wireless Communication

Robert Fromm$^{(\boxtimes)}$ (ID), Lydia Schott (ID), and Faouzi Derbel (ID)

Faculty of Engineering, Leipzig University of Applied Sciences (HTWK),
Wächterstraße 13, 04107 Leipzig, Germany
{robert.fromm,lydia.schott,faouzi.derbel}@htwk-leipzig.de
https://fing.htwk-leipzig.de/de/fakultaet/professuren/prof-faouzi-derbel

Abstract. For power-limited wireless sensor networks, energy efficiency is a critical concern. Receiving packages is proven to be one of the most power-consuming tasks in a WSN. To address this problem, the asynchronous communication is based on wake-up receivers. The proposed receiver circuit can detect on-off keying pulses inside the 868 MHz band with a sensitivity of -60 dBm. The power consumption of the circuit is only $3.6\,\mu W$. The circuit design is kept simple, only requiring commercial off-the-shelf components like general-purpose operational amplifiers and comparators.

Keywords: Wake-up receiver (WuRx) · Wireless sensor network (WSN) · Ultra-low power (ULP) · Collision avoidance · Carrier sensing · Energy detection · LF correlation · Passive RF architecture · Operational amplifier · Comparator · Schottky diode · Envelope detector

1 Introduction

The use of wireless sensor networks (WSNs) in research and industry is steadily increasing. WSNs are essential for the sensing and collection of environmental data in different application fields [9]. Powering sensor nodes using small batteries is often mandatory. Recharging and swapping batteries is usually not possible or would lead to higher maintenance costs. Parameters like latency, transmission range, and sensitivity are likewise major parameters when designing the hardware of a sensor node.

A continuous or a real-time wireless communication is nowadays essential for many applications when building an autonomous WSN. To maintain such a wireless communication even with modern wireless transceivers would lead to a power consumption greater than 10 mW. In order to power such a sensor node for a long period with a battery, the receiving and sending intervals need to

© Springer Nature Switzerland AG 2022
A. Ahrens et al. (Eds.): SENSORNETS 2020/2021, CCIS 1674, pp. 60–84, 2022.
https://doi.org/10.1007/978-3-031-17718-7_4

decrease significantly. This inevitably leads to increased latency and response times of the WSN.

A wake-up receiver (WuRx) is a special RF receiver that enables the sensor node to be in a continuous receiving mode. Different approaches with passive and active components exist in order to keep the WuRx's power consumption below $10\,\mu W$. Figure 1 shows how a WuRx can be integrated into a sensor node.

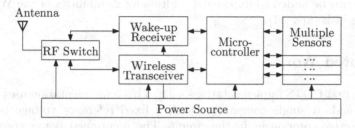

Fig. 1. A wireless sensor node with a WuRx based on [13]. A RF switch is used to separate both receiving paths of WuRx and wireless transceiver.

A sensor node is typically built out of antenna, wireless transceiver, sensors, energy source, and microcontroller. Due to the WuRx, a second RF reception path is introduced. Either the wireless transceiver receives data packets or the WuRx receives wake-up packets (WuPts). Multiple antennas can be used or an RF switch is introduced in order to switch between these two RF paths. The microcontroller takes care of the configuration of the WuRx. During standby, the WuRx is typically the only active component in the circuit. If a WuPt is received, the WuRx sends an interrupt to the microcontroller to wake up. [13].

The WuRx implementations are divided into two categories: application-specific integrated circuit (ASIC)-based WuRx and WuRx implemented using commercial off-the-shelf (COTS) components [17]. This paper will focus on the COTS implementations of WuRx, because of a much better repeatability of results, simpler, and cheaper implementations and integration of a WuRx in a commercial product. In Fig. 2 the typical building blocks of a COTS WuRx can be seen.

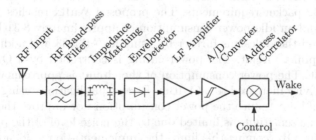

Fig. 2. Building blocks of a typical COTS WuRx with passive envelope detector.

The WuRx's input signal is characterized with low amplitude, high noise figure, and various interferences. Usually, an RF band-pass filter is used to pass only signals of the desired frequency bands. A passive envelope detector performs the signal detection and conversion to a LF signal. An impedance matching circuit is needed to avoid power losses through signal reflection from the envelope detector. The LF amplifier circuit is needed to boost the rectified signal to be detectable by the following analog-to-digital converter circuit. A digital address correlator can be added to implement addressing capabilities of the WuRx and avoid false wake-ups [11].

2   Related Work

One of the first COTS implementations is [3]. This implementation uses a passive RF front end. A single comparator with a fixed reference voltage is used as the only active component in the circuit. The mentioned power consumption of $2.6\,\mu W$ is interesting, but the sensitivity of the circuit can be expected as very low. The given maximum range is 10 m when using 868 MHz as the carrier frequency.

The implementation of [15] improves the previous implementation by introducing an adaptive threshold, adding further measurements and investigations. The performance of three different COTS comparators were investigated. The maximum sensitivity of −55 dBm was achieved with the LPV7215 with a power consumption of $1.2\,\mu W$. With comparator TLV3691, only −32 dBm and 152 nW were achieved.

Our implementation [11] added a base-band amplifier using COTS operational amplifiers (OAs). Signals up to −50 dBm can be detected reliably, but the power consumption increased to $4.2\,\mu W$. Further investigations were made, in order to use the circuit for both transmitter and receiver power savings.

[14] proposes a design with OA and comparator, that claims to reach a sensitivity of −70 dBm with a power consumption below $1\,\mu W$. This is possible due to a very slow data rate of approximately 20 bit/s, resulting in a huge power consumption of the wake-up transmitter (WuTx).

A different approach for implementing a WuRx lies in using a special integrated circuit acting as a LF WuRx. One of the first implementations is [13] using the AS3932. A specially modulated WuPt needs to be sent in order to fulfill the AS3932 packet requirements. The proposed WuRx reaches a sensitivity of −52 dBm and an idle power consumption of approximately $8.3\,\mu W$.

[7] improved these designs further by using an AS3933 and adding a power-gated LF amplifier circuit. The power-gating is controlled by a OA and comparator circuit. The power consumption of the circuit is approximately $7.3\,\mu W$ and the sensitivity increased to −61 dBm. Recent publications using the AS3933 like [8,12] could not reduce the power consumption nor improve the sensitivity.

The WuRx's sensitivity is limited due to the noise level of the passive diode detector circuit. Overcoming this limit, the implementation of [6] added a duty-cycled low-noise amplifier (LNA) resulting in a sensitivity of −90 dBm. During active phase, the power consumption reaches over 1 mW. Through duty-cycling an average power consumption of only $3\,\mu W$. Because of duty-cycling, the latency increases to 30 ms.

3   Theoretical Analysis

The different building blocks of a COTS WuRx are shown in Fig. 2. The following subsections describe and analyze them theoretically.

3.1   Envelope Detector's Diode Calculation

All the implementations [3, 6–8, 11–15] are using enveloped detectors with zero-biased Schottky diodes. Using diode based envelope detectors is one of the ways to passively demodulate an RF signal. While active mixer circuits are capable of demodulating multiple modulation types, envelope detector can only be used for amplitude-modulated signals, e.g. on-off keying (OOK) . The envelope detector consists of a non-linear element performing a rectification process. After low-pass filtering, only the LF parts of the signal remain.

The diode's open-circuit output voltage $V_{\text{out}}^{\text{OC}}$ can be modeled as a function of the incident RF power P_{in}. This function can be divided into two regions. A linear region for larger input powers with P_{in} proportional to $V_{\text{out}}^{\text{OC}^2}$ and the square-law region for smaller input powers with P_{in} proportional to $V_{\text{out}}^{\text{OC}}$. The limit of the square-law region can be seen in Eq. 1, with V_{T} the thermal voltage and n the diode's ideality factor [5, p. 585].

$$V_{\text{out}}^{\text{OC}} < nV_{\text{T}} \approx 26\,\text{mV}, \quad \text{with } n \approx 1, T = 300\,K \tag{1}$$

Because of low input powers in WuRx applications, the following analyses will be focused on the square-law region of the diode. Equation 2 is the definition of the open-circuit voltage sensitivity γ^{OC} [5, p. 568].

$$V_{\text{out}}^{\text{OC}} = \gamma^{\text{OC}} \cdot P_{\text{in}} \tag{2}$$

The diodes behavior can be modeled as a Thévenin equivalent, with the open-circuit voltage $V_{\text{out}}^{\text{OC}}$. The equivalent resistance is often called video resistance R_{v}. R_{v} is defined by the diode's series resistance R_{s} and the diode's junction resistance R_{j}, see Eq. 3 [5, p. 569].

$$R_{\text{v}} = R_{\text{s}} + R_{\text{j}} \tag{3}$$

Equation 4 is the formula of the diode's junction resistance, with I_{s} the diode's saturation current and bias current I_{DC}. $I_{\text{DC}} = 0$ for a zero-biased envelope detector [5, p. 566].

$$R_{\text{j}} = \frac{nV_{\text{T}}}{I_{\text{s}} + I_{\text{DC}}} \tag{4}$$

The open-circuit voltage sensitivity is calculated by Eq. 5 with C_j the diode's junction capacitance and $\omega_{carr} = 2\pi f_{carr}$ the RF carrier frequency [5, p. 574].

$$\gamma^{OC} = \frac{1}{2nV_T} \cdot \frac{R_j}{1 + \rho(1 + \nu^2)}, \quad \text{with } \rho = \frac{R_s}{R_j}, \nu = \omega_{carr} C_j R_j \tag{5}$$

The sensitivity of the diode for envelope detection is not only dependent on the voltage sensitivity, but also affected by the diode's noise figure. The diode's noise voltage is defined by the Johnson-Nyquist noise through the video resistance R_v. The Eq. 6 shows the calculation with k_B the Boltzmann constant and f_B the LF-signal bandwidth [5, p. 570].

$$V_n = \sqrt{4k_B T f_B R_v} \tag{6}$$

The tangential signal sensitivity (TSS) P_{TSS} is defined as the minimum RF power level, where the LF signal's amplitude is larger than the noise peak-to-peak value. The relationship of $V_{out}^{OC} = 2.8 \cdot V_n$ is used [5, pp. 570f].

$$P_{TSS} = \frac{2.8 \cdot \sqrt{4k_B T f_B R_v}}{\gamma^{OC}} \tag{7}$$

The diode HSMS-2852 from Agilent Technologies is the typical diode used in the envelope detector by many publications [3,7,12,14,15]. Because this diode is not any more provided by the manufacturer, an alternative is needed. The SMS7630-006LF from Skyworks Solution Inc. has nearly identical parameters and the following investigations were made, to ensure that the diode SMS7630 is a good alternative diode [11]. A theoretical analysis of the parameters defined in the previous equations was made. Table 1 shows the results.

Table 1. Comparison of HSMS-2852 and SMS7630 - calculated parameters [1,20].

Parameter	HSMS-2852	SMS7630
n	1.06	1.05
R_s	$25\,\Omega$	$20\,\Omega$
C_j	$180\,\mathrm{fF}$	$140\,\mathrm{fF}$
I_s	$3\,\mu A$	$5\,\mu A$
nV_t	$27.4\,\mathrm{mV}$	$27.1\,\mathrm{mV}$
R_j	$9.13\,\mathrm{k}\Omega$	$5.43\,\mathrm{k}\Omega$
R_v	$9.16\,\mathrm{k}\Omega$	$5.45\,\mathrm{k}\Omega$
γ^{OC}	$162\,\mathrm{mV}/\mu\mathrm{W}$	$98.1\,\mathrm{mV}/\mu\mathrm{W}$
P_{TSS}	$-76.7\,\mathrm{dBm}$	$-75.7\,\mathrm{dBm}$

$T = 300\,\mathrm{K}, f_{carr} = 868\,\mathrm{MHz}, f_B = 10\,\mathrm{kHz}$

The small parameters deviations result into slightly different values for R_j, R_v, and γ^{OC}. But the values for the TSS are nearly identical, resulting in an nearly equal performance of both diode types.

3.2   Envelope Detector Architecture

When designing an envelope detector, single or multiple diodes in different configurations can be used. Such diode rectifiers are typically used in RF energy harvesting applications [26]. It shall be noticed, that WuRx applications are faced to much lower RF input powers. Figure 3 shows a selection of the implementations utilized in WuRxs. Earlier implementations like [3] are utilizing a Dickson voltage multiplier and most of the current implementations like [6–8,11–15] use the Greinacher voltage doubler. The performance of a single-diode implementation shall be investigated.

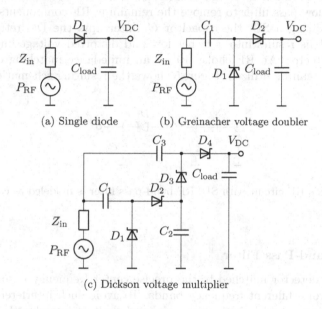

(a) Single diode   (b) Greinacher voltage doubler

(c) Dickson voltage multiplier

Fig. 3. A selection of envelope detector architectures utilized in WuRxs.

The performance of the single diode (SD) and voltage doubler (VD) circuit will be investigated through measurements. The performance of the corresponding architecture is highly dependent on the utilized impedance matching network. Because the diodes' impedance is typically not equal to the previous building block's output impedance, most of the signal power is reflected, resulting in a lower diode's output voltage.

3.3   Impedance Matching Circuit

Many impedance matching circuits for diode rectifier were investigated in the context of RF energy harvesting. Typically either strip lines or lumped components are used [26]. The selection of WuRx implementations [3,6–8,11–15] are utilizing an L-shaped network with one inductor and one capacitor. Figure 4 shows the resulting RF circuit when utilizing a VD.

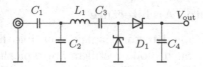

Fig. 4. WuRx's RF circuit with VD. RF band-pass filter is modeled as capacitor C_1.

The RF band-filter is modeled as C_1. The L-shaped LC matching is represented through the components C_2 and L_1. In order to fulfill a full-wave rectification for the Greinacher voltage doubler, C_3 is needed as a coupling capacitor. C_4 acts as a low-pass filter to remove the remaining RF components.

When utilizing a SD, the capacitor C_1 interrupts the DC return path of the circuit. This results into a rather low and distorted voltage output of the enveloped detector. An RF choke [19] or an impedance matching circuit with two inductors can be utilized. Figure 5 shows the resulting schematic.

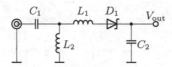

Fig. 5. WuRx's RF circuit with SD. RF band-pass filter is modeled as capacitor C_1.

3.4   RF Band-Pass Filter

An envelope detector matched to the precise center frequency is susceptible to RF signals from different frequency bands. To avoid such interferences, an RF band-pass filter of the desired frequency band shall be introduced. SAW filters allowing only a narrow-band transmission are available as COTS parts. Because of the insertion loss of the surface acoustic wave (SAW) filter, the output voltage of the envelope detector is reduced.

The utilized SAW filter B39871B3725U410 has a center frequency of 869 MHz, a bandwidth of 2 MHz, and a typical insertion loss of 2.5 dB [18]. Because of the envelope detector's square-law behavior, this leads to a reduction of the output voltage of 44 %. The decrease of the WuRx's sensitivity is equal to the filter's insertion loss, but the utilization of a SAW filter in a noisy real-live environment is essential.

3.5   LF Amplifier

The envelope detector's voltage output needs to be amplified in order to be detectable by the following A/D converter. OA are used as voltage amplifiers in implementations like [7,11,14]. [6] introduces a voltage amplifier with two bipolar junction transistors (BJTs).

Gain-Bandwidth Product. Supply current and gain bandwidth product (GBWP) are highly dependent on each other. Amplifiers with high GBWP are allowing high amplification factors while maintaining fast response time and high data rates. Figure 6 shows the GBWP and supply current of a selection of suitable COTS OAs. The implementation of [7] used ISL28194, [11] used TLV512, and [14] used LPV611.

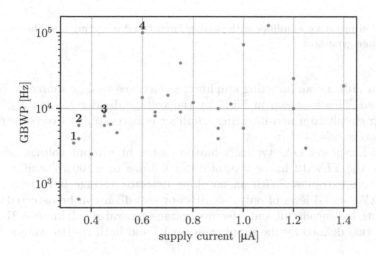

Fig. 6. GBWP and supply current of selection of operational amplifiers. Marked devices: 1) ISL28194, 2) TLV512, 3) LPV611, 4) MCP6141.

When choosing the right OA for the circuit, a trade-off between current consumption and reaction time has to be made. A lower current consumption means a lower GBWP. A low GBWP leads to a slow reaction time because of a slower settling time of the OAs. To convert the GBWP to the settling time t_{settle} the Eq. 8 can be used as an approximation. In Eq. 8 τ represents the time constant, ω_k the angular low-pass filter cut-off frequency, f_k the cut-off frequency, and A_F the voltage amplification factor [11].

$$t_{settle} \approx 3\tau = \frac{3}{\omega_k} = \frac{3}{2\pi \cdot f_k} = \frac{3 \cdot A_F}{2\pi \cdot \text{GBWP}} \qquad (8)$$

Operational Amplifier Circuit Design. In order to meet the power delivery restraints of a WSN, only a single-rail supply can be used for the amplifier circuitry. When designing an amplifier, the input and output signals must match the input and output voltage swings of the OA. Figure 7 shows inverting and non-inverting amplifier circuits with corresponding biasing circuits [22].

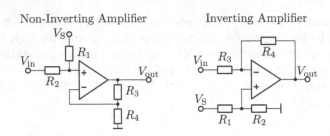

Fig. 7. Non-inverting amplifier with biasing circuit and inverting amplifier with reference voltage generator.

When utilizing an inverting amplifier, a reference voltage source needs to be introduced. This is shown in Fig. 7 by the voltage divider R_1 and R_2. Adding a biasing circuit to a non-inverting amplifier is necessary to overcome possible input voltage offsets.

Ultra-low-power OAs typically have a rather high input voltage offset. For instance, the TLV512 has a typical offset voltage of $\pm 100\,\mu V$ and $\pm 3\,mV$ at temperature extremes. With an envelope detector voltage sensitivity of $\gamma = 40\,mV/\mu W$, signal level of only $-56\,dBm$ or $-41\,dBm$ can be detected accordingly. Both biasing circuit and reference voltage generator will increase the power consumption defined by the supply voltage V_S and both resistor values R_1, R_2.

BJT Based Amplifiers. Previous simulations and experiments showed, that it is possible to use RF BJTs like the BFP405 as a low-power LF amplifier. Using an ultra low-current biasing circuit promising higher GBWPs and lower supply currents than OA circuits. A combination of a common-emitter and common-collector configuration is used because of its high voltage gain, high input impedance, and low output impedance. Figure 8 shows amplifier circuit.

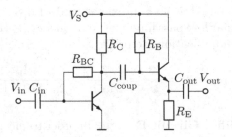

Fig. 8. Common-emitter and common-collector stage of a BJT based amplifier.

Simulations were used to optimize the component values according to the desired frequency response, gain, and current consumption. With $C_{in} = C_{coup} = C_{out} = 1\,nF$, $R_{BC} = R_B = 100\,M\Omega$, $R_C = 10\,M\Omega$, and $R_E = 5\,M\Omega$ a gain of 43 in the range of 500 Hz to 10 kHz was reached. The circuit's current consumption is around 530 nA.

3.6 Comparator Circuit

To make the analog output signal of the LF amplifier detectable to the digital address decoder, an analog-to-digital converter is utilized. The implementations [3,6,11,14,15] are utilizing comparator as 1 bit converters.

Input Offset Voltage. [15] compared the performance of the TLV3691, AS1976, and LPV7215 and stated that input offset voltage is the comparator's sensitivity-limiting factor. Many low-power comparators have a built-in input hysteresis, which is often higher than the typical input offset figure. The hysteresis is the minimum voltage difference on the comparator that needs to be overcome in order to latch the compactor output. Table 2 shows the performance of three low-power comparator circuits. TS880 was added because AS1976 is no longer COTS available. The minimum detectable signal (MDS) is the sum of input offset and hysteresis. The last row shows the theoretical WuRx's sensitivity if the comparator circuit is connected directly to the envelope detector.

Table 2. Comparison of multiple COTS comparators [2,21,23,24].

Parameter	TLV3691	AS1976	TS880	LPV7215
Supply current (typ.) [nA]	75	200	300	790
Propagation delay (typ.) [μs]	45	15	7	13
Input offset (typ.) [mV]	3	1	1	0.3
Input offset (max.)[a] [mV]	17	5	10	6
Hysteresis [mV]	17	3	2.6	0
MDS[b] [mV]	34	8	12.6	6
Sensitivity[c] [dBm]	−30.7	−37.0	−35.0	−38.2

[a]$T = 25\,°C$, [b]minimum detectable signal, [c]with $\gamma = 40\,mV/\mu W$

The sensitivity value of −55 dBm stated by [15] can only be reached if comparator's typical input offset applies. Input offset distribution charts like [23, Figure 21] show that the typical value only applies in a small proportion of the manufactured circuits. This makes the utilization of such a comparator in a commercial product unfeasible. The utilization of a LF amplifier circuit is inevitable.

Reference Generator. The implementations [3,7,11] are using a comparator with a constant reference voltage, typically generated by a voltage divider. [6,14, 15] are using an adaptive reference voltage generated by an RC circuit. Figure 9 shows the schematic of both implementations.

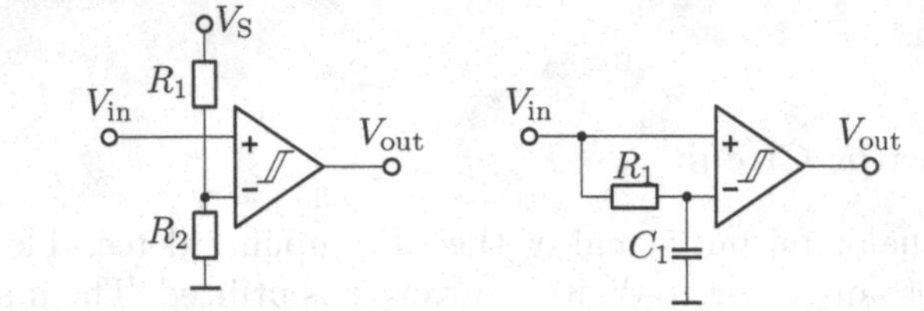

Fixed Reference Voltage   Adaptive Reference Voltage

Fig. 9. Fixed and adaptive reference generator for comparator circuit.

Using a fixed reference voltage leads to additional power consumption. While the fixed reference voltage's turn-on time is near zero, the adaptive reference voltage takes several milliseconds in order to charge C_1 to the correct voltage level. The adaptive reference level makes it easier to detect periodic square-wave signals, because the reference voltage is charged up to half of the signal amplitude. Fixed reference voltage makes it easier to detect single impulses in case of a carrier sensing implementation.

4   Experimental Analysis

4.1   Impedance Matching

Four different test printed circuit boards (PCBs) were built-up in order to investigate the envelope detector behavior. Table 3 shows the configuration of these PCBs, with [1] being the reference PCB, [2] utilizing the HSMS2852 diode, [3] utilizing the single diode (SD) configuration, and [4] with the SAW filter added.

Table 3. Configuration of the envelope detector test PCBs

PCB	Diode	Diode configuration	SAW filter
[1]	SMS7630-006LF	VD	No
[2]	HSMS2852	VD	No
[3]	SMS7630-079LF	SD	No
[4]	SMS7630-006LF	VD	B39871B3725U410

The components' values of the impedance matching network was derived from the simulation. Small adjustments were made in order to overcome additional parasities and set the center frequency as close as possible to 868 MHz. PCB [4] needed to be matching before the SAW filter was added. Figure 10 shows the reflection factor of PCB [1] and [4].

The reached reflection factor on PCB [1] is approximately $\Gamma_{[1]} = -15$ dB. The SAW filter creates a more narrow-band matching. The minimum refection factor is approximately $\Gamma_{[4]} = -10$ dB.

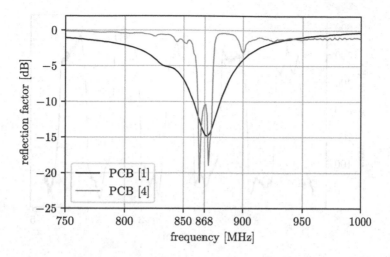

Fig. 10. Reflection factor of test PCB with [1] and without the SAW filter [2].

4.2   Envelope Detector

Voltage Sensitivity. With the following experiment the voltage sensitivity of four different envelope detector configurations (see Table 3) was measured. Figure 11 shows the block diagram of the measurement setup. The signal generator produced an OOK signal with a low frequency of 1 kHz. The power and carrier frequency of the signal generator can be varied. In order to make the small signal levels detectable by the oscilloscope, a differential LNA was added. The oscilloscope is measuring the signal amplitude due to a 1 kHz OOK-modulated signal. Figure 12 shows the envelope voltage of PCB [1] at an input level of −50 dBm. The measured signal amplitude is around 450 μV. The oscilloscope images of the other PCBs were nearly identical.

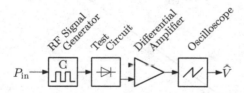

Fig. 11. Block diagram of the voltage sensitivity measurement.

Figure 13 shows the envelope voltage of each PCBs at multiple input power levels. The figure shows clearly the square-law behavior of the envelope detector for input levels lower −30 dBm and the linear behavior for input levels higher −20 dBm. The voltage sensitivity was averaged over the square-law region. PCB

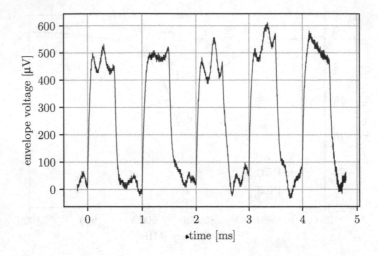

Fig. 12. Envelope voltage of PCB [1] at an input level −50 dBm.

[1] resulted into $\gamma_{[1]} = 45$ mV/μW, PCB [2] $\gamma_{[2]} = 58$ mV/μW, PCB [3] $\gamma_{[3]} = 28$ mV/μW, and PCB [4] $\gamma_{[4]} = 22$ mV/μW.

The calculated voltage sensitivity values could not be reached due to additional losses and mismatches. As calculated, the voltage sensitivity of the HSMS2852 is slightly higher than the SMS7630's. Using the SD configuration instead of a VD results into a lower input voltage even at low input levels. Adding the SAW filter halves the output voltage, due to an insertion loss of nearly 3 dB.

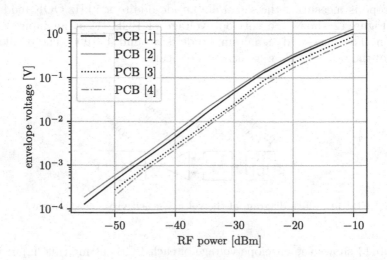

Fig. 13. Measurement of the voltage sensitivity of four test PCBs.

Video Resistance. Verifying and measuring the value of video resistance R_v is important to make sure, that the amplifier's input impedance does not lower the envelope voltage. The video resistance is the internal resistance of the Thévenin equivalent. Equation 9 shows the calculation of the video resistance, when measuring the open-circuit envelope voltage V_{out}^{OC} and the output voltage V_{out} with an additional load resistance R_L.

$$R_v = R_L \cdot \left(\frac{V_{out}^{OC}}{V_{out}} - 1 \right) \tag{9}$$

Table 4 shows the measurements and resulting video resistance. The measurements were made with an RF power of $-30\,\text{dBm}$ to ensure proper square-law region behavior. The calculated video resistance $R_{v,\text{calc.}}$ is derived from Table 1. The video resistance needs to be doubled when using the using a VD configuration.

Table 4. Measurements and calculations of the video resistance of the four test configurations.

PCB	V_{out}^{OC} [mV]	R_L [kΩ]	V_{out} [mV]	$R_{v,\text{meas.}}$ [kΩ]	$R_{v,\text{calc.}}$ [kΩ]
[1]	47.1	10	21.7	11.7	10.9
[2]	60.7	10	25.7	13.6	18.3
[3]	29.3	10	16.9	7.3	5.45
[4]	23.6	10	11.1	11.2	10.9

The comparison of the measured and calculated video resistances shows, that the measurements of PCBs [1] and [4] are a good match. The video resistance measurement of the PCB [3] utilizing the SD configuration is slightly too high. The measurement of PCB [2] utilizing the HSMS2852 diode is significantly to low. A video resistance of around 11 kΩ can be estimated for the configurations of PCB [1] and [4].

4.3   Comparator Performance Test

Based on the following experiment, the performance of different comparator circuits will be evaluated. The comparators TLV3691, TS881, and LPV7215 will be utilized and compared following the selection of [15]. Because the AS7619 is no longer available, the TS881 was introduced due to its similar specifications.

Figure 14 shows the utilized schematic of the test PCB. The RF front-end configuration [4] was used. The components R_1 and C_3 are forming the adaptive comparator threshold.

An 868 MHz RF signal with a 5 ms pulse every 100 ms was used to test the three comparators. Values of 1 MΩ and 10 nF were used for R_1 and C_3 accordingly. Both the RF front-end output and the comparator output were measured

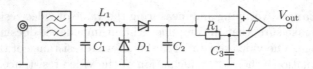

Fig. 14. Schematic of the comparator test PCBs with RF front-end according to PCB [4], comparator with adaptive threshold.

by an oscilloscope. This way the minimum signal amplitude, minimum RF level, and propagation delay can be measured. Table 5 shows the measurements results.

Table 5. Measurement results of comparator performance test.

Parameter	TLV3691	TS881	LPV7215
Calculated MDS[a,b] [mV]	34	12.6	6
Calculated sensitivity[b] [dBm]	−30.7	−35.0	−38.2
Propagation delay (typ.) [µs]	45	7	13
MDS[a] [mV]	21	4.5	0.54
Minimum RF level [dBm]	−31	−38	−47
Propagation delay [µs]	80	8	28

[a]minimum detectable signal, [b]see Table 2

The TLV3691 circuit detected a signal of −31 dBm and the TS881 of −38 dBm. These results are quite similar to the calculated from Table 2. For smaller signals, the comparator output stayed at a constant signal level. The comparator's hysteresis prevents unwanted signal changes through interferences or noise.

The test circuit utilizing the LPV7215 was able to detect a signal down to −47 dBm. Because LPV7215 has no internal hysteresis, the input offset voltage is the only limiting factor. This leads to interferences triggering the comparator output if a low input signal is present.

4.4   LF Amplifier Test

The following experiments are used to investigate the performance of amplifier circuits in detail. Three different amplifiers were built up and their performance is measured. The first two are OA-based designs. Amplifier [1] is utilizing the ultra-low-power TLV521 [25]. Amplifier [2] is utilizing the non-unity-gain-stable OA MCP6141 with a very high GBWP and a low power consumption [16]. Amplifier [3] is built up using two transistors BFP405 in a common-emitter and common-collector configuration. Table 6 summarizes the most important specifications of these three designs.

Table 6. LF amplifier test circuits [16, 25].

Parameter	[1]	[2]	[3]
Amplifier type	OA-based	OA-based	BJT-based
OA/BJT	TLV521	MCP6141	BFP40
Current consumption (typ.)	350 nA	600 nA	—
GBWP (typ.)	6 kHz	100 kHz	—
Input offset (max.)	3 mV	3 mV	—
Gain setting	×200	×30	—
Bandwidth (calc.)	30 Hz	3.3 kHz	—
Biasing current consumption	300 nA	300 nA	530 nA
Total current consumption	650 nA	900 nA	530 nA

All three designs were built up. To verify the frequency behavior of the amplifier circuits the gain was measured in the range of 10 Hz to 20 kHz. Figure 15 shows the frequency response of the three amplifier circuits.

As expected, the first two amplifier circuits have a low-pass filter's frequency response. Amplifier [1] has a very low cut-off frequency. The cut-off frequency of amplifier [2] is around 1 kHz. Amplifier [3] has a band-pass filter's frequency response due to the coupling capacitors allowing the transistor's biasing. This amplifier is reaching a higher upper frequency with a lower current consumption than the other amplifiers.

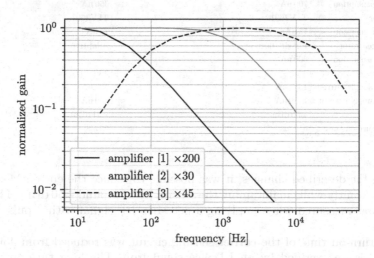

Fig. 15. Measurement results of the frequency response of the three amplifier circuits.

5 Proposed Circuits

5.1 Carrier Sensing Circuits

The main idea of a carrier sensing circuit is the implementation of a very simple WuRx. This WuRx is only capable of detecting a single RF pulse in order to wake-up the main RF transceiver. Additional applications lie in a channel busy assessment in order to avoid transmission collisions.

Proposed Circuits. The first proposed circuit was introduced in [11]. This design was further improved resulting, into a new and better implementation. The following changes were made. The biasing circuit was integrated into the first amplifier stage. The amplification factor can be reduced due to fewer losses inside the biasing circuit. This leads to the possibility to use only one amplification stage. An adaptive threshold generation is used to further reduce the current consumption. In Table 7 compares these two implementations in detail.

Table 7. Comparison of carrier sensing circuits.

Parameter	Implementation [11]	Improved implementation
Biasing circuit	Additional voltage divider with high-pass filter	Integrated into first amplifier stage
Current consumption	300 nA	300 nA
LF amplifier	Dual-stage non-inverting	Single-stage non-inverting
OA	2× TLV521	1× TLV521
Total gain	900	200
Current consumption	700 nA	350 nA
Comparator	TLV3691	TLV3691
Current consumption	75 nA	75 nA
Reference generator	Fixed: 100 mV	Adaptive
Current consumption	300 nA	—
Supply voltage	3 V	3 V
Calculated supply current	1375 nA	725 nA
Measured supply current	1400 nA	860 nA
Sensitivity	−50 dBm	−51 dBm
Simulated turn-on time	450 ms	50 ms

With the described changes, it was possible to reduce the current consumption significantly while maintaining the sensitivity at around −50 dBm. This sensitivity was measured when applying a 868 MHz RF signal with a pulse length of 5 ms.

The turn-on time of the carrier sensing circuit was reduced from 450 ms to 50 ms. This was verified by an LTspice simulation. The long turn-on time of the old implementation is due to additional high-pass filter, that were needed in order to remove the additional offsets by the biasing circuit and input offsets of the OAs. The filter's time constant needed to be set accordingly in order to prevent signal distortion of the 5 ms carrier pulse.

Usability as a Wake-Up Receiver. To test the usability of the circuit as a wake-up receiver, a radio transceiver module is used. A carrier pulse at the center frequency of 868 MHz at the output power of 11 dBm is generated. Two $\lambda/2$ whip antennas are used for the transmitter and the carrier sensing test circuit. With this setup, a maximum transmission range of around 10 m can be observed [11].

Interferences of other RF systems are present. Especially Wi-Fi transmitter are capable of bypassing the SAW filter due to high transmission powers. Designing a carrier sensing circuit with a sensitivity greater -50 dBm is not effective, because these interferences occur more and more frequently. Additional filtering criteria need to be introduced.

Usability as a Carrier Sensing Circuit. The second usage is found in carrier detection and collision avoidance techniques. When communicating in a wireless network, package collision is quite frequent. These collisions lead to an energy loss because the current package needs to be resent.

Modern wireless transceiver modules often have a carrier sensing circuit, clear channel assessment module, or wake-on radio integrated. The improvement is much better sensitivity, and selectivity. But when taking a look at typical current consumption of these modes, they are in the order of 10 mA [4]. The comparison of this current consumption to the current consumption of the proposed circuit shows that an improvement of factor 10.000 can be achieved [11].

5.2 Low Frequency Correlator

Working Principle. Because of multiple RF sources in a real-life environment, the carrier sensing circuit is not sufficient to act as a reliable WuRx. With higher sensitivity false-positives occur more often. With lower sensitivity the WuPt's reception range decreases. A simple implementation to receive WuPts more reliable is to detect a special frequency inside the demodulated signal. This way, a OOK-modulated signals with a special LF signal needs to be transmitted and detected by the WuRx.

For the LF correlation, the serial or universal asynchronous receiver transmitter (UART) interface of a MSP430G2553 is used. A symmetrical square-wave signal with a specific frequency can be interpreted as a valid UART signal. With the start bit being a logical 0 and stop bit a logical 1 a square wave signal results into the received hexadecimal value of 55_{16}. Figure 16 shows the interpretation of a square-wave signal as an UART signal. In order to match the receiver's timing constrains the bit duration T_{bit} must be exactly the half of the square wave's period T_{SW}.

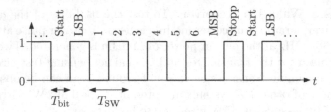

Fig. 16. Interpretation of a symmetrical square-wave as a valid UART signal. T_{bit} being the bit duration and T_{SW} the period of the square-wave signal.

To save energy, only low-power clock sources can be used. Using a clock crystal with a frequency of 32.768 kHz leads to an MSP430's current consumption of 700 nA. It has to be noted, that running a clock crystal oscillator inside a wireless sensor node is often mandatory for timers and real-time clocks. That is why the following power consumption figures will not include the MSP430's power needs.

The baud rate of the UART receiver is configured by a clock divider n. The minimum clock divider is $n = 3$ resulting to a baud rate of 10.92 kHz and a square-wave frequency of 5.46 kHz. Due to lower frequency responses of the utilized amplifiers lower bit rates will be utilized.

Proposed Circuits. In the following section, two different implementations of a WuRx utilizing the LF correlator will be investigated. Figure 17 shows these two implementations and Table 8 lists the parameters in detail. The amplifier circuits [2] and [3] see Table 6 were used. The comparator LPV7215 was utilized due to its low current consumption and high sensitivity. The time constant of the adaptive reference generator's low-pass filter was set to $\tau = 1$ ms. The circuits' settling times were simulated with LTspice. The BJT-based implementation's settling time is significantly higher due to the amplifier circuit's coupling capacitors. Measures to decrease the settling time would either distort the signal or increase the current consumption.

Sensitivity Measurements. The comparator output signal of the circuit is fed into the MSP430's input pin of the UART module. The UART module is configured to the specified correlation frequency. If a valid UART symbol is received by the MSP430, an interrupt is executed. If the received UART symbol is equal to 55_{16}, an output pin is set, signaling a successful WuPt reception. According to Fig. 16 more than five OOK pulses are needed in order to receive a valid UART symbol. For the following sensitivity measurements, a WuPt is defined as 12 OOK pulses. Figure 18 shows the block diagram of the sensitivity measurement setup.

The test circuit and MSP430 are connected to the RF signal generator. A special counter circuit is build up in order to enable the RF generator to send

Fig. 17. Photography of the two proposed circuits [2] and [3] implemented on test PCBs with WuRx RF front-end. Additional RF shielding can be applied for final sensitivity tests.

Table 8. Comparison of LF correlator circuits.

Parameter	Proposed circuit [2]	Proposed Circuit [3]
Amplifier	OA-based [2][a]	BJT-based [3][a]
Current consumption	900 nA	530 nA
Amplification	×30	×45
Cut-off frequency	≈3 kHz	≈10 kHz
Comparator [24]	LPV7215	LPV7215
Current consumption (typ.)	790 nA	790 nA
Propagation delay (typ.)	13 s	13 s
Total current consumption (calc.)	1.69 A	1.32 A
Total current consumption (meas.)	1.6 A	1.2 A
Simulated settling time	200 s	30 ms

[a] see Table 6

WuPts and count the WuPt detected by the MSP430. By comparing sent and received packet counts the packet error rate (PER) can be estimated.

Because the amplifier circuit [2] is limited to 3 kHz, a baud-rate divider of $n = 16$ was selected, resulting into a baud rate of 2048 Hz and a square-wave frequency of 1024 Hz. With 12 OOK pulses, the WuPt duration is 11.7 ms. The input power of the RF signal generator was varied in the range of −45 to −65 dBm, $N = 1000$ packets were transmitted, and the PER was estimated.

Figure 19 shows the resulting sensitivity curves of both designs. The design [2] receives the majority of the WuPts down to −55 dBm. The design [3] reaches around −60 dBm.

Because the amplifier of design [3] is capable to amplifying higher-frequency signals, a baud-rate divider of $n = 4$ with a baud-rate of 8192 Hz and a square-wave frequency of 4096 kHz was tested. With $n = 4$ the WuPt with 12 OOK pulses is only 2.93 ms. Figure 20 shows the sensitivity curves at different correla-

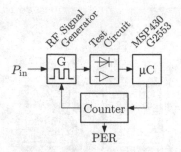

Fig. 18. Block diagram of the WuRx's sensitivity measurement.

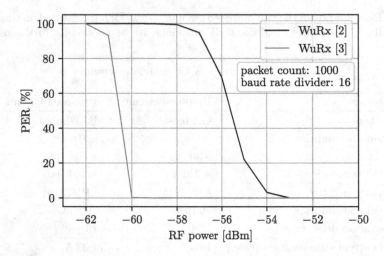

Fig. 19. Packet error rate vs. input power comparing OA-based design [2] and BJT-based design [3].

tion frequencies. Due to the higher frequency the sensitivity drops from $-60\,\mathrm{dBm}$ to $-56\,\mathrm{dBm}$.

Usability as a Wake-Up Receiver. To test the usability of the circuit as a WuRx, the same test procedure described in previous subsection was used. An RF transmitter with a power of $11\,\mathrm{dBm}$ and two $\lambda/2$ whip were used. With this setup, higher transmission ranges even through obstacles like walls could be achieved. Interferences from other RF systems could not be observed.

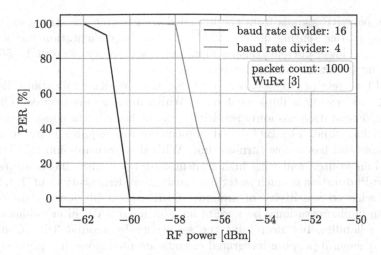

Fig. 20. Packet error rate vs. input power of the BJT-based design [3] comparing slow ($n = 16$) and fast ($n = 4$) data rates.

6 Discussion

6.1 Further Work

The proposed circuits show a simple way to implement WuRx without any specialized integrated circuits. The circuit's RF path is kept simple. Further investigations shall be made in order to find out, whether the theoretical values of the voltage sensitivities can be reached. The OA-based LF amplifier was optimized successfully in comparison to the publication [11]. Non-inverting OA circuit with integrated biasing depletes the OA's capabilities completely while enabling a fast settling time. The comparator's adaptive threshold generation works reliable.

Currently, the circuit was only built for a carrier frequency of 868 MHz. By swapping the SAW filter and matching the RF circuit other frequency bands can be used. Further tests will be made to test the circuit's performance in the 433 MHz and 2.45 GHz range. According to Friis' transmission formula [10] the transmission loss of the RF signal is dependent on the wavelength resulting into higher transmission ranges when utilizing the 433 MHz band. The 2.45 GHz range is highly important due to its capability to realize high data rate transmissions.

Further work is needed to implement an address correlator in the LF correlator circuits. The microcontroller's UART module can be used to implement the data reception. Manchester encoding can be used in order to ensure a 50 % duty cycle and proper workings of the adaptive reference generator.

6.2 Usability as a Wake-Up Receiver

The carrier sensing circuit proposed in Subsect. 5.1 can be used as a WuRx in shielded areas or areas with low RF activities. One application of high importance in future is a vibration measurement system inside a metal gear box. In this case only RF signals from the intended transmitter are strong enough to excite the carrier sensing circuit. The improved implementation has a faster turn-on time, lower current consumption, and a sensitivity of around −50 dBm. This circuit is suitable for the intended use case.

The LF correlator circuits are suitable for many WuRx applications. Because no WuRx addressing is implemented, all WuRx in range are excited. The OA-based implementation has lower sensitivity and higher current consumption, but faster settling time. The BJT-based implementation requires more additional components and has a slow turn-on time. With slow transmission rate WuPt of only 11.7 ms is used and with high transmission rate only 2.93 ms are needed. These WuPt duration is much faster than current implementations of [7,8,12,14].

The achieved sensitivity of around −60 dBm is a bit lower than current always-on implementations, because of an additional SAW filter enhancing the circuit's reliability, but decreasing the sensitivity by around 3 dB. Compared to [7] only general-purpose integrated circuits are used, lowering the costs, and making the search for replacement parts easy.

6.3 Conclusion

In this work a power-saving approach with energy detection and carrier sensing is presented. The proposed circuit utilizing the 868 MHz band was improved resulting into a sensitivity of −50 dBm, a power consumption of 2.6 μW, and a settling time of 50 ms. The maximum observed transmission range is around 10 m.

To further improve the sensitivity of this circuit, a LF correlator was added in order to differentiate wake-up packets from interferences. An implementation based on operational amplifiers and another implementation based on bipolar junction transistors was introduced. The sensitivity was increased up to −60 dBm with a power consumption of 3.6 μW. Further tests will be made in order to utilize these circuits in different frequency bands like 433 MHz or 2.45 GHz.

Acknowledgment. This work is financially supported by Leipzig University of Applied Sciences by funds of Sächsisches Staatsministerium für Wissenschaft, Kultur und Tourismus.

References

1. Agilent Technologies: Agilent HSMS-285x SeriesSurface Mount Zero Bias Schottky Detector Diodes, June 2005. (datasheet)
2. ams AG: AS1976. AS1977 Ultra-Low Current, 1.8 V Comparators (2007). (datasheet)
3. Ansari, J., Pankin, D., Mähönen, P.: Radio-triggered wake-ups with addressing capabilities for extremely low power sensor network applications. Int. J. Wirel. Inf. Netw. **16**, 118–130 (2008). https://doi.org/10.1007/s10776-009-0100-6
4. Atmel: AT86RF233 - Low Power, 2.4GHz Transceiver for ZigBee, RF4CE, IEEE 802.15.4, 6LoWPAN, and ISM Applications (2014)

5. Bahl, I., Bhartia, P.: Microwave Solid State Circuit Design. Wiley, New York (2003)
6. Bdiri, S., Derbel, F., Kanoun, O.: A tuned-RF duty-cycled wake-up receiver with −90 dbm sensitivity. Sensors **18**(1), 86 (2018). https://doi.org/10.3390/s18010086,https://www.mdpi.com/1424-8220/18/1/86
7. Bdiri, S., Derbel, F., Kanoun, O.: A wake-up receiver for online energy harvesting enabled wireless sensor networks: technology, components and system design, pp. 305–320. De Gruyter Oldenbourg, November 2018. https://doi.org/10.1515/9783110445053-018
8. Cabarcas, F., Aranda, J., Mendez, D.: OpenWuR - an open WSN platform for WuR-based application prototyping. In: Proceedings of the 2020 International Conference on Embedded Wireless Systems and Networks on Proceedings of the 2020 International Conference on Embedded Wireless Systems and Networks, pp. 212–217. EWSN 2020, Junction Publishing, USA (2020)
9. Chee-Yee Chong, Kumar, S.P.: Sensor networks: evolution, opportunities, and challenges. Proc. IEEE **91**(8), 1247–1256 (2003). https://doi.org/10.1109/JPROC.2003.814918
10. Friis, H.T.: A note on a simple transmission formula. Proc. IRE **34**(5), 254–256 (1946). https://doi.org/10.1109/JRPROC.1946.234568
11. Fromm, R., Schott, L., Derbel., F.: An efficient low-power wake-up receiver architecture for power saving for transmitter and receiver communications. In: Proceedings of the 10th International Conference on Sensor Networks - SENSORNETS, pp. 61–68. INSTICC, SciTePress (2021). https://doi.org/10.5220/0010236400610068
12. Galante-Sempere, D., Ramos-Valido, D., Lalchand Khemchandani, S., del Pino, J.: Low-power RFED wake-up receiver design for low-cost wireless sensor network applications. Sensors **20**(22), 6406 (2020). https://doi.org/10.3390/s20226406, https://www.mdpi.com/1424-8220/20/22/6406
13. Gamm, G.U., Sippel, M., Kostic, M., Reindl, L.M.: Low power wake-up receiver for wireless sensor nodes. In: 2010 Sixth International Conference on Intelligent Sensors, Sensor Networks and Information Processing, pp. 121–126 (2010). https://doi.org/10.1109/ISSNIP.2010.5706778
14. Kazdaridis, G., Sidiropoulos, N., Zografopoulos, I., Korakis, T.: eWake: A Novel Architecture for Semi-Active Wake-Up Radios Attaining Ultra-High Sensitivity at Extremely-Low Consumption (2021)
15. Magno, M., et al.: Design, implementation, and performance evaluation of a flexible low-latency nanowatt wake-up radio receiver. IEEE Trans. Indus. Inf. **12**(2), 633–644 (2016). https://doi.org/10.1109/TII.2016.2524982
16. Microchip: MCP6141/2/3/4 - 600 nA, Non-Unity Gain Rail-to-Rail Input/Output Op Amps (2019). (datasheet)
17. Piyare, R., Amy.L.Murphy, Kiraly, C., Tosato, P., Brunelli, D.: Ultra low power wake-up radios: a hardware and networking survey. IEEE Commun. Surv. Tutor. **19**, 2117–2157 (2017). https://doi.org/10.1109/COMST.2017.2728092
18. RF360 Europe GmbH: SAW RF filter - B39871B3725U410 (2019). (datasheet)
19. SkyWorks Inc.: Mixer and Detector Diodes, August 2008. https://www.skyworksinc.com/search?q=200826a
20. Skyworks Solutions Inc: Surface-Mount Mixer and Detector Schottky Diodes, June 2018. (datasheet)
21. STMicroelectronics NV: TS881 - Rail-to-rail 0.9 V nanopower comparator, December 2013. (datasheet)
22. Texas Instruments: Single-Supply Op Amp Design Techniques, Mar 2001. (Application report)

23. Texas Instruments: TLV3691 0.9-V to 6.5-V, Nanopower Comparator, November 2015. (datasheet)
24. Texas Instruments: LPV7215 Micropower, CMOS Input, RRIO, 1.8-V, Push-Pull Output Comparator, August 2016. (datasheet)
25. Texas Instruments: TLV521 NanoPower, 350nA, RRIO, CMOS Input, Operational Amplifier, May 2016. (datasheet)
26. Tran, L.-G., Cha, H.-K., Park, W.-T.: RF power harvesting: a review on designing methodologies and applications. Micro Nano Syst. Lett. 5(1), 1–16 (2017). https://doi.org/10.1186/s40486-017-0051-0

Seismic Sensor Network for High Density Deployments: Concept, Design, Deployment and Results

Marco Manso[1]([envelope])([iD]), Mourad Bezzeghoud[1,2], José Borges[1,2], and Bento Caldeira[1,2]

[1] Instituto de Ciências da Terra, Universidade de Évora, Évora, Portugal
marco@marcomanso.com
[2] Departamento de Física (ECT), Instituto de Ciências da Terra (IIFA), Universidade de Évora, Évora, Portugal

Abstract. The devastating impact that seismic events can cause to societies demands that the underlying physical processes that cause them are better understood. Seismic networks have been increasingly deployed over the years allowing to measure ground motion with great accuracy and, in a few cases, reaching high-density deployments for high-resolution measurements. In this chapter it is described the work conducted to build a high-density seismic network comprised of low-cost network-enabled accelerometer sensors to monitor the Alentejo region. The design resulted in a modular platform that can operate with different sensors. Following a noise performance evaluation, the Analog ADXL355 accelerometer was selected for the deployment phase. Herein, sensor system measurements were compared with a professional seismometer, using two actual seismic events recorded in Portugal. These events allowed to demonstrate the sensors capabilities in detecting weak (2.5 ML) to moderate (3.4 ML) seismic events at short (8 km) and medium (140 km) distances respectively. Comparing obtained measurements with a professional seismometer, however, the sensor prototypes exhibited, as expected, a higher presence of sensor noise. Overall it is concluded that the sensor system has a potential application in seismology.

Keywords: High-Density Seismic Network · Seismic Sensors · MEMS · Accelerometers · Seismology · Sensor noise

1 Introduction

Seismic events can be extreme and severely threat whole societies, causing a high death toll, victims and property damage. Taking as a recent example, the 2004 Sumatra Earthquake and Tsunami in Indian Ocean started with an undersea earthquake with a magnitude of 9.1, generating a tsunami that devastated "coastal areas as far away as East Africa. [...] The tsunami killed at least 225,000 people across a dozen countries, with Indonesia, Sri Lanka, India, Maldives, and Thailand sustaining massive damage." [1] The Iberian Peninsula and the North of Africa - part of the Ibero-Maghrebian region between the Gulf of Cadiz and Algeria – also register the occurrence of large earthquakes

© Springer Nature Switzerland AG 2022
A. Ahrens et al. (Eds.): SENSORNETS 2020/2021, CCIS 1674, pp. 85–103, 2022.
https://doi.org/10.1007/978-3-031-17718-7_5

since they share the Eurasian–Nubian plate boundary that corresponds to a well-defined narrow band of seismicity [2].

Helping to understand the physical processes that cause earthquakes, seismic networks, capable to measure ground motion in great accuracy, have been deployed in increasing number. Portugal, in particular, has made a significant effort to develop the Broadband Portuguese seismic network integrating seismological stations from various institutions supporting real-time monitoring of the earthquake activity [3, 4]. Between 2010 and 2012, the West Iberia Lithosphere and Asthenosphere Structure (WILAS) project integrated a temporary network of 20 sensors in the Portuguese national network resulting in a total of 55 stations spaced on average by 50 km [5, 6]. These stations continuously recorded measurements at frequencies up to 100 Hz, thus collecting a large volume of high-quality data of densely distributed broadband stations [7]. More recently, the Arraiolos seismic network (in Alentejo) was deployed comprising 14 broadband stations (CMG 6TD, 30s) of the Institute of Earth Sciences of Évora, Portugal (Instituto de Ciências da Terra or ICT) and temporarily extended with 21 short-period stations (CDJ, 2.0 Hz) of the Dom Luiz Institute of Lisbon, Portugal (Instituto Dom Luiz or IDL) within a 20 km radius [4, 8].

In the continued endeavor to increase seismic monitoring resolution by deploying more seismic stations, researcher have exploited recent technological innovations applied to sensors and sensor platforms covering increased performance, reduced energy consumption, improved connectivity, miniaturization and reduced cost. Combined together, these innovations enable the deployment of large sensor networks for "live" (online and real-time) monitoring of seismic activity with high spatial resolution [9], as well as with the potential to identify precursor signals associated with earthquakes [10], a capability that can be used for Early-Warning applications and thus to alert populations and reduce the time to respond to a disaster. It is herein presented a few cases of high-density seismic sensor deployments:

a) **Sensor Network deployed in the Long Beach Area:** During 2011, more than 5200 high-frequency (10-Hz corner frequency) velocity sensors, with an average spacing close to 100m, were deployed in the Long Beach area as part of a petroleum industry survey [11]. The main purpose was to better define the area, including construction of a high-resolution 3D shallow crustal structure. The Long Beach high-density deployment was a pioneering effort that demonstrated the high-resolution observation and reconstruction of seismic activity.

b) **University of Southern California's (USC) Quake-Catcher Network (QCN):** is a seismic network that implements distributed/volunteer computing with the potential to provide critical earthquake information by filling in the gaps between traditional seismic stations [12]. Initially, it started to exploit data produced by accelerometers pre-installed in computers and now uses USB-connected Microelectromechanical systems (MEMS) accelerometers and mobile-phone accelerometers. The system communicates via the Berkeley Open Infrastructure for Network Computing (BOINC) [13]. QCN can only record strong motion and requires a connected computer to operate.

c) **CalTech's Community Seismic Network (CSN):** established by 2009, consists in an earthquake monitoring system based on a dense array of low-cost acceleration sensors aiming to produce block-by-block measurements of strong shaking during an earthquake[1]. In 2015, CSN was described as a 500 element network located in the Los Angeles area of California in the USA [14]. The expansion plan throughout the Los Angeles region consists in deploying sensors in schools by involving the Los Angeles Unified School District (LAUSD). The expansion started with 100 schools and was later supplemented with additional 200 campuses. The plan is to reach all 1000 campuses of LAUSD and extend to other public and private schools in the region (4000 campuses in total).

d) **MyShake Platform: Leveraging on Mobile Phones:** The MyShake Platform is an operational framework to provide earthquake early warning (EEW) to people in earthquake-prone regions. It is built on existing smartphone technology to detect earthquakes and issue warnings [15]. Over 300,000 people around the globe have downloaded the MyShake app, however the number of active users (i.e., active phones connected) only peaked at 25k.

e) **SSN Alentejo:** The Seismic Sensor Network Alentejo (SSN-Alentejo) developed by ICT brings the most dense seismic sensor network ever deployed in Portugal. This novel network aims to improve the characterization of seismic activity in the region and to improve earthquakes' assessment. Planned for 2020 and 2021, SSN-Alentejo will deploy a monitoring network of 60 sensors to generate significant volumes of live data and advance seismology knowledge. The sensors will be distributed in a mesh configuration spaced on average 10 km and covering an area of about 5000 square kilometers.

The evolution of the seismic network in Arraiolos and planned deployments for SSN-Alentejo are presented in Fig. 1 [16].

The remainder of this chapter is organized as follows: Sect. 2 presents the potential application of MEMS accelerometers for seismology, including their advantages and limitations; Sect. 3 describes the sensor system designed and built for seismological applications, incorporating MEMS accelerometers and network-enabled capability. The section also describes work conducted to evaluate the noise present in several MEMS accelerometers, while measuring at rest, which allows to identify the most appropriate accelerometers for seismic operations. Importantly, the developed method can also be applied on-site and in-operation, to determine the occurrence of seismic events. Section 4 present results of deploying and testing a MEMS sensor system (defined in Sect. 3) with the ADXL355 accelerometer, including results obtain from two recorded seismic events in Portugal, using a reference seismic station for comparison purposes. Section 5 presents the main conclusions of the paper, also outlining future possible work.

---

[1] http://csn.caltech.edu.

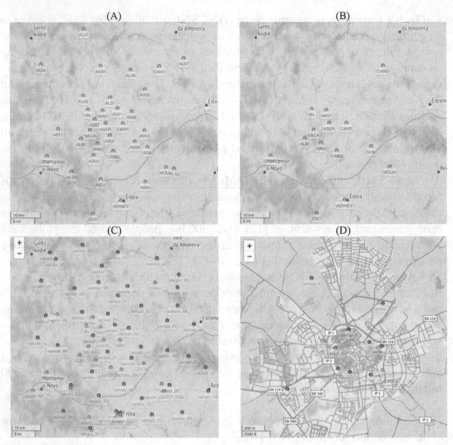

Fig. 1. Different phases of the seismic network in Alentejo (includes the Arraiolos region) and the SSN-Alentejo planned deployment. (A) Temporary seismic network deployed in the Arraiolos region after the earthquake. About 60 connected stations. (B) Current seismic network in the Arraiolos region. Less than 15 connected stations. (C) SSN-Alentejo: planned deployment of additional 60 sensors, resulting in about 75 stations in total. (D) SSN-Alentejo: planned deployment for the Évora city. Sensor density is increased to monitor ground motion activity that may impact cultural heritage and historical buildings [16]. The SSN-Alentejo project is funded by the Science Foundation of Portugal (FCT) under grant number ALT20–03-0145-FEDER-031260.

2 MEMS Accelerometers for Seismology

The evolution in sensors and sensing network technology has brought improvements in performance (resolution, sensibility and processing capacity), operation (energy efficiency, operation time) and connectivity (broadband communications), at a significant cost reduction [17]. Low-cost MEMS accelerometers, in particular, demonstrated the capability to generate relevant data for seismic analysis in dense deployment contexts [18]. MEMS technology has enabled the mass production of small size accelerometers. Capacitive accelerometers, in particular, are highly popular due to reduced cost, their simple structure, and the ability to integrate the sensor close to the readout electronics.

When subjected to an acceleration, the inertial mass shifts cause a proportional change in capacitance. By measuring the capacitance change, the acceleration can be calculated.

For purposes of seismology and as presented by Manso *et al.* [9], state-of-the-art low-cost MEM-based accelerometers:

a) provide adequate sensitivity, noise level, and range (measured in g) to be applicable to earthquake strong-motion acquisition (M > 3.0), thus also limiting the "resolution" capability. However, the high level of instrumental self-noise that increases as frequency decreases limits their application in the study of low frequency weak-motion forces [19, 20];
b) are well fit to measure high frequency (>40 Hz) ground motion [20] since their resonant frequency (typically above 1 kHz) is far above the seismic band pass;
c) measure the gravity acceleration component that provides a useful reference for sensitivity calibration and tilt measurement;
d) have high acceleration ranges (several g) and are capable to sustain high acceleration (several hundred g) without being damaged;
e) when compared with seismometers, such as geophones, may have an advantage in detecting weak high frequency signals, while geophones may have the advantage in detecting weak signals at low frequencies;
f) can have useful applications such as Earthquake Early Warning System (EEWS), seismic hazard map and security applications [21].

As the underlying technologies to build connected MEMS systems became more accessible and affordable, several efforts are currently using dedicated MEMS sensors to build dense seismic sensor networks, as the case of CSN and the urban MEMS seismic network in the Acireale Municipality (Sicily, Italy) [22]. They have found several fields of application, including: seismological study and earthquake observation, seismic activity monitoring networks, and seismic surveys [23].

3-axis MEMs accelerometers are already used to augment existing seismic networks, essentially filling in the gaps between higher-quality sensors [24]. Furthermore, MEM technology will surely continue to evolve and it is expected that their performance on weak low frequency signals will improve.

3   The Network-Enabled Seismic Sensor System

Presented in [25], the authors developed a prototype for a seismic system using a MEMS accelerometer connected to a microcontroller. The system operates autonomously, is network enabled and is capable to deliver high data throughput. The sensor system is presented next. Note that three different sensors were used for evaluation purposes (Table 1).

Table 1. Seismic sensor system architecture components.

Component	Architecture component see [25]
ESP8266	Acquisition and processing board (32-bit processor at 80 MHz); Storage (internal flash, between 512 KiB and 16 MiB); Networking (integrated TCP/IP protocol stack, Wi-Fi)
TDK InvenSense MPU-6050 or ST LIS3DHH or Analog ADXL355	MEMS accelerometer
Internal clock synchronised with NTP	Real-time clock

For the Acquisition and Processing Board, the ESP8266 is selected because it provides: a fast and programmable microcontroller (operates at 80 or 160 MHz); Storage capabilities (embedded flash up to 4 MiB); Networking capabilities (via its embedded Wi-Fi chip). RTC time synchronisation is achieved by means of Network Time Protocol (provided by a NTP server). The ESP8266 also supports a wide range of libraries, in large part provided by the Arduino community.

Concerning the accelerometer, three different components were integrated: MPU-6050, LIS3DHH and ADXL355.

The sensor system overview including components' interconnections are presented in Fig. 2. The pin connections between the components are presented in figure. Note that the depicted accelerometer is the MPU-6050. The data interface used is the I2C Digital Interface (Table 2).

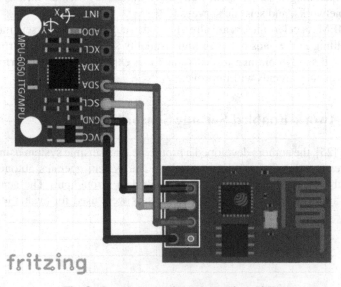

Fig. 2. Sensor system interconnections [25].

Table 2. Sensor system interfaces [25].

Interface	ESP Pin	Sensor Pin
I2C	Pin 0	SDA
I2C	Pin 2	SCL

The sensor system was designed to rely in existing network and power infrastructure. In this regard, the design did not seek power consumption optimisation.

3.1 Noise Performance Comparison

Section 2 introduced MEMS accelerometers, describing their application for seismology, also mentioning as a main limitation the presence of sensor noise that is originated from the sensor's electrical and mechanical components. In this subsection, an indication of sensor noise, first described in [17], is measured by deploying and collecting acceleration data, while at rest position, from the different sensors used in the sensor system.

The sensor noise assessment is made by calculating the standard deviation of the signal (calculated using a "moving window" of 100 samples). The lower the standard deviation the lower the sensor noise.

The standard deviation is calculated using the well know formula 1:

$$\sigma = \sqrt{\frac{\sum (x_i - \mu)^2}{N}} \tag{1}$$

where:
i is the sample number,
x_i is the measurement related with sample i,
μ is the mean value and.
N is the sample size.

The environment where accelerometers are installed might be affected by external factors (e.g., traffic or seismic activity), which can be registered by accelerometers and should be excluded from the sensor noise analysis. In order to exclude these "signals" from "noise", a threshold logic is defined and implemented as follows:

```
let σ(n) be the standard deviation related with sample window n
let σmin be the registered minimum standard deviation for the running
    period

if ( σ(n) > σmin . Threshold ) then
    is signal
else
    is noise
endif
```

The following devices were analysed:

- A TCL mobile phone
- A Xiaomi mobile phone
- A CAT mobile phone
- TDK InvenSense MPU-6050 (used in the sensor system)
- ST LIS3DHH (used in the sensor system)
- Analog ADXL-355 (used in the sensor system)

The results are presented next.

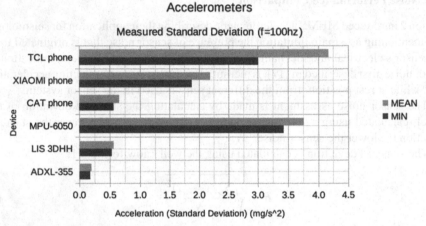

Fig. 3. Measured standard deviation for several accelerometers operating at a sampling rate of 100 Hz [17].

Table 3. Measured standard deviation for several devices: minimum recorded value and mean value [17].

Device	σ_{MIN} (mg)	σ_{MEAN} (mg)
TCL phone	3.0115	4.1707
XIAOMI phone	1.8716	2.1893
CAT phone	0.5595	0.6563
MPU-6050	3.4253	3.7606
LIS 3DHH	0.5270	0.5634
ADXL-355	0.1734	0.1950

The developed method yields an indication of sensor noise, which is sensor specific. As shown in Fig. 3 and Table 3, the dedicated accelerometer ADXL-355 yields the lowest minimum standard deviation (0.1734 mg), followed by the LIS 3DHH (0.5270 mg), the CAT phone (0.5595 mg). The TCL phone and the MPU-6050 yield the highest values, with 3.0115 mg and 3.4253 mg respectively. It is also pertinent to note the disparity between the mean and the minimum value of standard deviation for the TCL phone, indicating that the minimum value for standard deviation alone is not sufficiently robust to assess sensor noise in actual deployments.

The presented analysis of sensor noise observed in different types of accelerometers, successfully developing a method to measure noise on-site and in-operation. The method produces an indication of sensor noise based on the measured standard deviation. It yields results consistent with sensors specifications (i.e., ADXL-355, LIS 3DHH and MPU-6050) or, when not available, with the observations. Importantly, the method adapts to the sensor's characteristics (e.g., sensor noise), allowing to identify the occurrence of relevant events (i.e., presence of signal), without necessarily knowing *a-priori* the sensor specification (noise is calculated with the sensor in-operation). In addition, this method also adapts to changing circumstances, such as "noise" alterations caused by subtle changes in sensor characteristics (resulting from e.g., small displacements or temperature change). When considering a high-density deployment, logistic and maintenance aspects can represent serious bottlenecks unless the system supports adaptive capabilities, as those here described.

4 Deployment and Trials

The MEMS sensor system configured with ADXL355 was deployed in University of Évoras' MITRA site shown in Fig. 4, at a 12 km distance of the city of Évora, that hosts the EVO station, a "Streckeisen STS-2/N" high performance seismometer, that will be used as the reference instrument to compare measurements obtained with the developed MEMS sensor system.

Fig. 4. Location of EVO station at MITRA site.

The MEMS sensor system was installed on 28th July 2020. The sensor is connected to a server hosted by the University of Évora. The sensor sends the measurement readings in real-time to the server using a Wi-Fi Access Point at MITRA.

During the trial phase, it was possible to monitor and detect seismic activity using the developed prototypes, specifically:

a) Event 1: Magnitude 3.4 (ML) with epicentre about 8 km east of Loures (Lisbon district), recorded 18-03-2021 at 9 h 51 (local time) (source: https://www.Ipma.pt/pt/geofisica/comunicados/, accessed 27-March-2021)
b) Event 2: Magnitude 2.5 (ML) with epicentre about 8 km north of Viana do Alentejo (about 10 km from EVO station) recorded 24-March-2021 at 14 h 30 (local time) (source: https://www.ipma.pt/pt/geofisica/comunicados/, accessed 27-March-2021)

4.1 Event 1: Magnitude 3.4 (ML) Recorded 18-March-2021 at 9 h 51 (Local Time)

The Portuguese Institute of the Sea and Atmosphere (IPMA) reported a seismic event with 3.4 magnitude (ML) and epicentre 8 km east of Loures (Lisbon district) that occurred at the 18-March-2021 around 9 h 51 (local time)[2]. The location of the event epicentre, as well as the MEMS sensor system (SSN), is presented in Fig. 5 (source: IPMA website, accessed 27-March-2021).

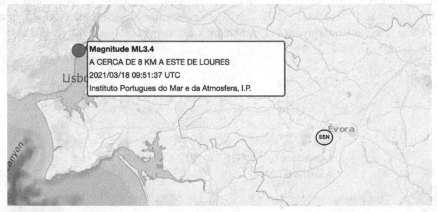

Fig. 5. Location of the seismic event with 3.4 magnitude (ML) with epicentre 8 km east of Loures (Lisbon district) reported by IPMA. The location of the MEMS sensor system is presented in the SSN circle. The MEMS sensor system is located at a distance of about 140 km from the epicentre.

The event was recorded by EVO station, as presented in Fig. 6, showing the arrival of the P-wave close to 9:51:54 (bottom).

---

[2] When the event occurred, Portuguese local time was the same as UTC time.

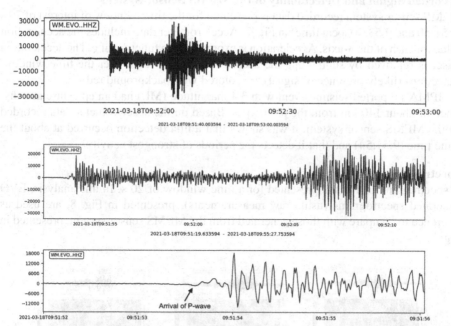

Fig. 6. EVO recording in the Z axis (HHZ) of a 3.4 magnitude event that occurred at March-2021 for a 100 s time window (top), a 60 s time window (middle) and a 4 s window (bottom). The figure's Y-axis shows the raw amplitude value as recorded by EVO. The P-wave is detected close to 9:51:53 (bottom), followed by the start of the S-wave close to 9:52:05. At 9:53:00, EVO still records level of ground activity above what was recorded before the event. [26].

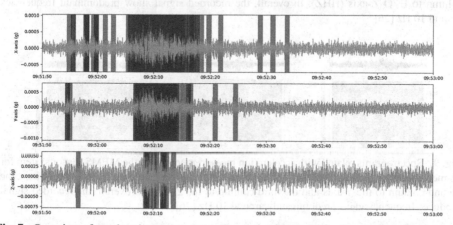

Fig. 7. Overview of acceleration measurements over the three axes for the sensor system over a 70 s time window (9:51:50 and 9:53:20 local time). The X-axis recorded the highest amount of ground motion activity. First detections start at about 9:51:54. The period with strongest activity starts at 9:52:05 continuing until 9:52:15 (the X-axis continues until 9:52:20). In overall, the presence of sensor noise does not allow observing presence of weak signals after 9:52:20 [26]. (Color figure online)

Recorded Signal and Detectability of the MEMS Sensor System

MEMS sensor system recorded data is presented for the time-window of interest of 70 s (9:51:50 and 9:53:30 local time) in Fig. 7. Accelerometer data includes the acceleration value for each of the 3-axis. Acceleration is expressed as a function of g. The acceleration offset is removed by subtracting the acceleration mean value over the time window. Detections (likely presence of signal) are colored with background red.

IPMA's reported seismic event with 3.4 magnitude (ML) had an epicentre at a distance of about 140 km from the prototypes. Based on the accelerometer data recorded by the MEMS sensor system, it was shown that a first detection occurred at about the same time (9:51:54) and that it detects the periods of strongest activity.

Spectrogram

A spectrogram analysis is presented for a time window of 20 s. In this analysis, EVO generated spectrograms (using raw measurements), presented in Fig. 8, are used as reference to compare with those generated from the MEMS sensor system, presented in Fig. 9.

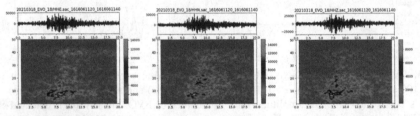

Fig. 8. Spectrograms related with EVO raw measurements for a time window of 20 s. The first column refers to EVO X-axis (HHE), the second column to EVO Y-axis (HHN) and the third column to EVO Z-axis (HHZ). In overall, the recorded signal show predominant frequencies around 10 Hz [26].

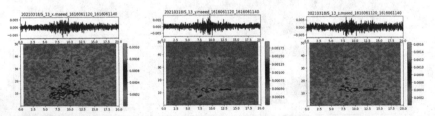

Fig. 9. Spectrograms related with acceleration measurements from the MEMS sensor system for a time window of 20 s (9:52:00 and 9:52:20 local time). The first column refers to the X-axis, the second column to the Y-axis and the third column to the Z-axis. In overall, the recorded signal produces frequency gains predominantly around 10 Hz [26].

In the X-axis, close to the region of maximum signal intensity (10 s), dominant frequencies cluster around 10 Hz (10 Hz is also dominant over time). The high dispersion in signal frequencies indicate presence of noise.

In the Y-axis, close to the region of maximum signal intensity (10 s), the dominant frequency is 10 Hz.

In the Z-axis, close to the region of maximum signal intensity (10 s), the dominant frequencies cluster around 10 Hz (10 Hz is also dominant over time).

The analysis in the frequency domain provides additional insights concerning the observation of the event of interest. The spectrograms generated from EVO raw measurements show that the recorded signal show predominant frequencies around 10 Hz in all X-Y-Z axes. Compared with EVO, the MEMS sensor system exhibit a higher dispersion of signal across several frequencies (being sensor noise a cause), yet there is a dominance of the 10 Hz frequency across all axis.

4.2 Event 2: Magnitude 2.5 (ML) Recorded 24-March-2021 at 14 h 30 (Local Time)

IPMA reported a seismic event with 2.5 magnitude (ML) and epicentre 8 km north-northwest of Viana do Alentejo (Évora district) that occurred at the 24-March-2021 around 14 h 30 (local time)[3]. The location of the event epicentre, as well as the MEMS sensor system (SSN), is presented in Fig. 10 (source: IPMA website, accessed 27-March-2021).

Fig. 10. Location of the seismic event with 2.5 magnitude (ML) with epicentre 8 km north-northwest of Viana do Alentejo (Évora district) reported by IPMA. The location of the MEMS sensor system is presented in the SSN circle. The MEMS sensor system is deployed at a distance of about 10 km from the epicentre.

The event was recorded by EVO station, as presented in Fig. 11, showing the start of the event close to 14:29:39 (bottom) in an increase in ground motion activity after 14:29:41. It is noted that the event time recorded by the EVO station is before IPMA's reported time at 14:30:13. Subsequent analysis concluded that EVO time synchronisation (based on the GPS module) was not operating correctly.

---

[3] When the event occurred, Portuguese local time was the same as UTC time.

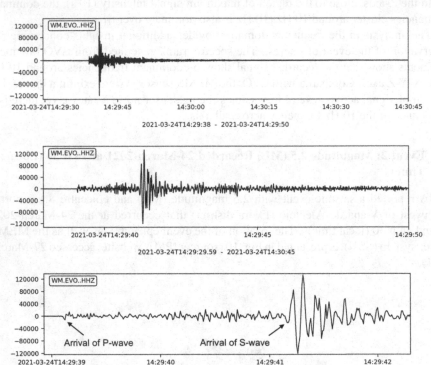

Fig. 11. EVO recording in the Z axis (HHZ) of a 2.5 magnitude (ML) for a 45 s window (top), a 12 s time window (middle) and a 3 s window (bottom). The figure's Y-axis shows the raw amplitude value as recorded by EVO. The event starts with the arrival of the P-wave at 14:29:39 (bottom), followed by the S-wave at about 14:29:41. At 14:30:00 (top), EVO still records ground activity above what was present before the event[26].

Recorded Signal and Detectability of the MEMS Sensor System

Recorded accelerometer data is presented for the time-window of interest of 20 s (14:30:15 and 14:30:35 local time). Accelerometer data includes the acceleration value for each of the 3-axis. Acceleration is expressed as a function of g. The acceleration offset is removed by subtracting the acceleration mean value over the time window. Detections (likely presence of signal) are colored with background red. It is noted that, since the time window in this subsection differs from the previous one (that used a time window of one hour), detections might differ.

IPMA's reported a seismic event with 2.5 magnitude (ML) had an epicentre at a distance of about 10 km from the prototypes. Based on the accelerometer data recorded by the MEMS sensor system, it was shown that the event was detected after 14:30:15 being active for most of the time window (especially in the X-axis) (Fig. 12).

Observations indicate that the MEMS sensor system is capable to detect the event.

Moreover, it is important to note that the time of the event, as reported by IPMA, is at 14:30:13, while the EVO station identifies first activity occurring at 14:29:39 (with its strong activity recorded between 14:29:41 and 14:29:43). The sensor prototypes report

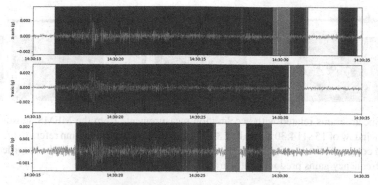

Fig. 12. MEMS sensor system acceleration measurements over a 20 s time window (14:30:15 and 14:30:35 local time). Detections are marked with a 'red' vertical rectangle. The event is detected in all axis after 14:30:16, with strongest amplitude above 2 mg for all axes. The X-axis exhibits the highest acceleration amplitude and detection over time [26]. (Color figure online)

the event as occurring between 14:30:17 and 14:30:25. Given the gap between EVO reported time of the event and IPMA's (that is closer to the sensor prototypes reported time), subsequent analysis concluded that EVO time synchronisation (based on the GPS module) was not operating correctly.

Spectrogram

A spectrogram analysis is presented for a time window for a time window of 15 s. In this analysis, EVO generated spectrograms (using raw measurements), presented in Fig. 13, are used as reference to compare with those generated from the MEMS sensor system, presented in Fig. 14.

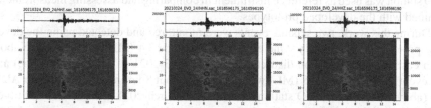

Fig. 13. Spectrograms related with EVO raw measurements for a time window of 15 s. The first column refers to EVO X-axis (HHE), the second column to EVO Y-axis (HHN) and the third column to EVO Z-axis (HHZ). In overall, the recorded signal show predominant frequencies around 10 Hz (in the X and Z EVO axis) and 10 Hz, 20 Hz, 30 Hz and 35 Hz in the Y-axis (EVO HHN) [26].

In the X-axis, close to the region of maximum signal intensity (close to 4 s), dominant frequencies cluster around 10 Hz and spread up to 40 Hz (10 Hz dominates over time). The high dispersion in the presence of frequencies indicate presence of noise. In the Y-axis, close to the region of maximum signal intensity (close to 4 s), dominant frequency is 10 Hz (10 Hz is also dominant over time). In the Z-axis, close to the region of maximum

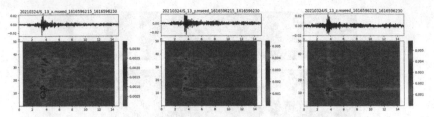

Fig. 14. Spectrograms related with acceleration measurements from the MEMS sensor system for a time window of 15 s (14:30:15 and 14:30:30 local time). The first column refers to the X-axis, the second column to the Y-axis and the third column to the Z-axis. In overall, the recorded signal produces frequency gains predominantly around 10 Hz [26].

signal intensity (close to 4 s), dominant frequency is 10 Hz (10 Hz is also dominant over time).

The spectrograms generated from EVO raw measurements show that the recorded signal show predominant frequencies around 10 Hz in the X and Z EVO axis (HHE and HHZ) and 10 Hz, 20 Hz, 30 Hz and 35 Hz in the Y-axis (HHN). Compared with EVO, the MEMS sensor system exhibit a higher dispersion of signal across several frequencies (being sensor noise a cause) however it is also visible a dominance of the 10 Hz frequency in X-axis and Z-axis, and 10 Hz, 20 Hz, 30 Hz and 35 Hz in the Y-axis (HHN) (for all sensors).

4.3 Findings

In this section, it was presented the results of field trials involving the MEMS sensor system using the ADXL355 sensor. The prototypes were installed in the MITRA site that hosts the EVO station, a "Streckeisen STS-2/N" high performance seismometer. The EVO station was used as reference instrument in comparing and assessing measurements obtained with the developed prototypes.

During this work, two seismic events were monitored and detected using the developed prototypes, specifically: One event of Magnitude 3.4 (ML) with epicentre about 8 km east of Loures (Lisbon district), recorded 18-03-2021 at 9 h 51 (local time) and one event of Magnitude 2.5 (ML) with epicentre about 8 km north of Viana do Alentejo (about 10 km from EVO station) recorded 24-March-2021 at 14 h 30 (local time). These events allowed to demonstrate the sensors capabilities in detecting weak (2.5 ML) to moderate (3.4 ML) events at short (10 km) and medium (140 km) distances, respectively. Comparing with the EVO professional seismometer, however, the sensor prototypes exhibited a higher presence of sensor noise.

5   Conclusion and Future Work

In this chapter it has been addressed the potential for high-density networks for seismic monitoring aiming to improve the resolution of the recorded seismic activity and consequently improving our understanding of the physical processes that cause earthquakes, as well of obtaining more detailed seismic characterisation of studied regions.

It was identified that MEMS technology, used to produce small size accelerometers, has a potential application in seismology. Indeed, MEMS accelerometers have enabled the deployment of high-density seismic networks capable to monitoring seismic activity with high spatial resolution. Example of high-density networks include CalTech's Community Seismic Network (CSN), MyShake Platform and SSN-Alentejo, the latter in deployment phase.

In this context, this chapter described the work conducted to design and deploy low-cost seismic sensor systems, based on low-cost MEMS accelerometers. The sensor system selected for deployment used the ADLX 355 accelerometer. A high-performance seismic station was used as reference sensor for comparison.

During field deployment and evaluation two seismic events were monitored and detected. These events allowed to demonstrate the sensors capabilities in detecting weak to moderate events at short and medium distances.

The following main conclusions can be drawn:

- The architecture herein defined has been demonstrated to be effective in the development and implementation of a MEMS sensor system. The architecture delivers real-time sensor data globally accessible over the Internet.
- Low-cost MEMS accelerometers are effective in detecting strong motion events. From the assessed MEMS accelerometers, the ADXL355 is the best performing, being expected to detect earthquakes with $M = 3$ and $M = 5$ at a distance larger than 10 km and 100 km respectively.
- Low-cost MEMS accelerometers exhibit high levels of self-noise well above Peterson's NHNM, limiting their application in seismology to moderate and strong motion events.
- Low-cost MEMS accelerometers exhibit characteristics that complement seismometers, given their high range and high natural frequency. MEMS accelerometers can be installed next to seismometers, providing additional insights concerning seismic activity and seismology in general.

In order to improve the sensor network capabilities, a few areas for improvement are suggested to be addressed in future work:

- The used low-cost MEMS accelerometers exhibit higher amplitude values and lower damping than those recorded by reference station EVO. Signal processing could be applied to make MEMS measurements closer to EVO.
- The sensor system measurements exhibit bias, which needs to be corrected before they can be used. Techniques for in-field calibration could be developed reducing burden for a large sensor network.
- Time synchronisation needs to be improved, either by using better techniques based on NTP or by incorporating highly accurate time sources like GPS.
- Combine multiple sensors operating as a single logical sensor, improving overall data quality by performing data analytics and correlation and obtain a class-A sensor (comparable to traditional seismometers).

While current MEMS accelerometers performance limits their application in seismology, it is expected that next generation MEMS accelerometers will generate reduced electronic self-noise and will improve frequency response, especially for low frequencies (below Hz), thus capable to compete with traditional seismometers and eventually becoming the *de facto* technology in seismology.

Acknowledgements. The SSN-Alentejo project is funded by the Science Foundation of Portugal (FCT) under grant number ALT20-03-0145-FEDER-031260 with the support of the Instituto de Ciências da Terra of the University of Évora (ICTUÉ) under the projects UIDB/04683/2020 and UIDP/04683/2020.

References

1. Rafferty, J.P.: The 6 Deadliest Earthquakes since 1950. Encyclopedia Britannica. https://www.britannica.com/list/6-deadliest-earthquakes. Accessed 2 Oct 2021
2. Ousadou, F., Bezzeghoud, M.: Seismicity of the Algerian tell atlas and the impacts of major earthquakes. In: Bendaoud, A., Hamimi, Z., Hamoudi, M., Djemai, S., Zoheir, B. (eds.) The Geology of the Arab World—An Overview. SG, pp. 401–426. Springer, Cham (2019). https://doi.org/10.1007/978-3-319-96794-3_11
3. Caldeira, B., et al.: Recent improvements in the broadband seismic networks in Portugal. EMSC Newsl. **22**, 18–19 (2007)
4. Carrilho, F., et al.: The Portuguese national seismic network—products and services. Seismol. Res. Lett. **92**(3), 1541–1570 (2021). https://doi.org/10.1785/0220200407
5. Veludo, I., et al.: Crustal seismic structure beneath Portugal and southern Galicia (Western Iberia) and the role of Variscan inheritance. Tectonophysics, 717, 16 October 2017, pp. 645–664 (2017)
6. Custódio, S., et al.: Ambient noise recorded by a dense broadband seismic deployment in Western Iberia. Bull. Seismol. Soc. Am. **104**(6), 2985–3007 (2014). https://doi.org/10.1785/0120140079
7. Palomeras, I., et al.: Finite-frequency Rayleigh wave tomography of the western Mediterranean: mapping its lithospheric structure. Geochem. Geophys. Geosyst. **15**(1), 140–160 (2014)
8. Wachilala, P., Borges, J., Caldeira, B., Matias, L., Rio, I., Bezzeghoud, M.: Characterization of the Region of Arraiolos, South Portugal – Period of January–May 2018. Ass. IUGG 2019, Montreal, Canada (2019)
9. Manso, M., Bezzeghoud, M., Caldeira, B.: Design and evaluation of a high throughput seismic sensor network. tools for planning, deployment and assessment. In: 6th International Conference on Sensor Networks SENSORNETS, Porto, Portugal, 19–21 February (2017)
10. Marco, M., Silva, H., Bezzeghoud, M.: PLASMA - a high-performing and open platform for the integration of heterogeneous sensor networks. In: Fifth Meeting of Post-Graduation in Physics and Earth Sciences of University of Évora, 21–22 September 2011
11. Inbal, A., Clayton, R., Ampuero, J.: Imaging widespread seismicity at midlower crustal depths beneath Long Beach, CA, with a dense seismic array: evidence for a depth-dependent earthquake size distribution. Geophys. Res. Lett. **42**(15), 6314–6323 (2015)
12. Cochran, E., Lawrence, J., Christensen, C., Chung, A.: A novel strong-motion seismic network for community participation in earthquake monitoring. IEEE Instru. Meas. Mag. **12**(6), 8–15 (2009)

13. Anderson, D.P.: BOINC: a system for public-resource computing and storage report. In: 5th IEEE/ACM International Workshop on Grid Computing, Pittsburgh, Pennsylvania, 8 November 2004

14. Clayton, C., Heaton, T., Kohler, M., Chandy, M., Guy, R., Bunn, J.: Community seismic network: a dense array to sense earthquake strong motion. Seismol. Res. Lett. **86**(5), 1354–1363 (2015). https://doi.org/10.1785/0220150094

15. Allen, R.M., Kong, Q., Martin-Short, R.: The myshake platform: a global vision for earthquake early warning. Pure Appl. Geophys. **177**(4), 1699–1712 (2019). https://doi.org/10.1007/s00024-019-02337-7

16. Manso, M., Bezzeghoud, M., Borges, J., Caldeira, B., Abdelhakim, A.: High-density seismic network for monitoring Alentejo region (Portugal) and Mitidja basin region (Algeria). Arab. J. Geosci. **13**(976), 2020 (2020). https://doi.org/10.1007/s12517-020-05972-w

17. Manso, M., Bezzeghoud, M.: On-site sensor noise evaluation and detectability in low cost accelerometers. In: 10th International Conference on Sensor Networks SENSORNETS, Online streaming, 9–10 February 2021

18. Lainé, J., Mougenot, D.: A high-sensitivity MEMS-based accelerometer. Lead. Edge. **33**, 1234–1242 (2014). https://doi.org/10.1190/tle33111234

19. Evans, J., et al.: Performance of several low-cost accelerometers. Seismol. Res. Lett. **85**(1), 147–158 (2014)

20. Farine, M., Thorburn, N., Mougenot, D.: General Application of MEMS Sensors for Land Seismic Acquisition – Is it Time? (2003). http://cseg.ca/assets/files/resources/abstracts/2003/218S0130.pdf

21. Pakhomov, A., Pisano, D., Sicignano, A., Goldburt, T.: Testing of new seismic sensors for footstep detection and other security applications. In: Sensors, and C3I Technologies for Homeland Security and Homeland Defense IV. Proceedings of SPIE, vol. 5778. SPIE, Bellingham, WA (2005) doi: https://doi.org/10.1117/12.604005

22. D'Alessandro, A., Luzio, D., D'Anna, G.: Urban MEMS based seismic network for post-earthquakes rapid disaster assessment. Adv. Geosci. **40**, 1–9 (2014)

23. Scudero, S., D'Alessandro, A., Greco, L., Vitale, G.: MEMS technology in seismology: A short review. In: 2018 IEEE International Conference on Environmental Engineering (EE). 12–14 March 2018. Milan, Italy (2018). https://doi.org/10.1109/EE1.2018.8385252

24. Evans, J., Hamstr, R., Spudich Jr, P., Kündig, C., Camina, P., Rogers, J.: TREMOR: A Wireless, MEMS Accelerograph for Dense Arrays. U.S. Department of the Interior, U.S. Geological Survey. Open-file Report 03–159 (2003)

25. Comunicações Geológicas: Contributor with article Design and Implementation of a Network Enabled High-Throughput MEMs-based Seismic Sensor. Comunicações Geológicas. **103**(1), 107–111 (2016). ISSN: 0873–948X; e-ISSN: 1647–581X

26. Manso, M.: Design and Prototyping of a Network-Enabled Low-Cost Low-Power Seismic Sensor Monitoring System (Doctoral dissertation). Universidade de Évora, Évora, Portugal (2021)

Acquisition of EFS and Capacitive Measurement Data on Low-Power and Connected IoT Devices

Julian von Wilmsdorff[1]([⊠]), Malte Lenhart[2], Florian Kirchbuchner[1],
and Arjan Kuijper[1]

[1] Fraunhofer Institute for Computer Graphics Research IGD, Darmstadt, Germany
{julian.von.wilmsdorff,florian.kirchbuchner,
arjan.kuijper}@igd.fraunhofer.de
[2] Technische Universität Darmstadt, Darmstadt, Germany
malte.lenhart@stud.tu-darmstadt.de

Abstract. In this extended version of the paper "Linoc: A Prototyping Platform for Capacitive and Passive Electrical Field Sensing" [15], the Linoc prototyping toolkit is presented in more detail, accompanied by evaluations and recent adaptations in research projects. Central to the Linoc Toolkit are the two capacitive and the two Electric Potential Sensing (EPS) groups, two technologies used for unobtrusive proximity detection in the field of Human Computer Interface (HCI). Important design goals in its creation were its usability and connectivity to facilitate future adaptation in research and the development of novel use cases. The usability and quality of the measurements of the Linoc prototyping toolkit were evaluated in terms of demonstration, usage and technical performance. Participants in the usage study expressed an interest for further usage, along with a fast learning curve. Technical benchmarks show a sensor range equal to its predecessors and several operational prototypes indicated its potential to be used in future projects. Consequently, first larger adaptations are presented in this paper. In addition to the presentation of the toolkit, we will also discuss the influence of the board firmware regarding noise generation and stability of the acquired capacitive and passive electric field measurements. The main focus of this investigation will be placed on peripherals of the microcontroller as well as parts of the prototyping platform that are capable of generating high frequency wave forms. These explorations of the capabilities of the toolkit are especially important for applications using the integrated Wi-Fi and Bluetooth modalities. Another complement in this extended version, is a more extensive description of the test setup used to measure the sensor performance to facilitate replication and confirmation of our results.

Keywords: Electric field sensing · Capacitive sensing · Electric potential sensing · Sensor · Sensor toolkit · Development board · Rapid prototyping · Embedded programming

1 Introduction

Not only since the Covid-19 pandemic have researchers discovered the value of contactless interactions. Besides being able to reduce infectious spread and saving doctors

© Springer Nature Switzerland AG 2022
A. Ahrens et al. (Eds.): SENSORNETS 2020/2021, CCIS 1674, pp. 104–124, 2022.
https://doi.org/10.1007/978-3-031-17718-7_6

Fig. 1. Front and back of the Linoc prototyping toolkit. Graphic from [15].

time to disinfect hands and surfaces, it can also be used to integrate smart behavior into everyday objects, such as lamps, tables, floors, carpets or doors to name only a few. The most interesting aspect for researchers is the design and evaluation of such new concepts. A lot of time however has to be spend on setting up sensors and measurement stands, until data can be acquired and further processed (Fig. 1).

Toolkits can accelerate this process by providing interfaces to sensors, or better yet, incorporating the sensor itself, thereby eliminating the need of programming skills and knowledge of intra-board bus protocols. Important properties of toolkits are ease of use, performance and versatility. Various specialized toolkits exist in different fields.

The Linoc prototyping toolkit, as first published in [15], is designed for easy data acquisition and to be easily integrated in future projects. The requirements for the hard- and firmware of the Linoc prototyping toolkit are thus designed to support ease of usage while allowing further refinement for advanced use cases. The main features are the integrated capacitive and passive Electric Potential Sensing (EPS) sensor groups, which are primarily intended for activity, proximity and/or movement detection. Both sensor types have different strength and weaknesses and can hence be selected according to the ambient environment and application. As we designed the toolkit as a sensor platform, we assume that most signal processing takes place at a computational more powerful endpoint, so that changes of the Linoc firmware are rarely necessary. If at a later project stage it is decided to transform the successful prototype into a standalone product, the modular firmware design allows easy integration of custom code. Only at this point in the design phase the user then has to be able to program for embedded systems.

A special feature of the Linoc toolkit is the ability to form sensor arrays by connecting multiple boards to a sensor network. One primary device will aggregate sensor data of multiple nodes, before posting them to the host computer via USB, or to server via a wireless connection.

This paper is structured as follows. A brief overview of related toolkits in the Human Computer Interface (HCI) proximity detection field is given in Sect. 2. Section 3 details the design process and its implementation in hard- and firmware of the Linoc toolkit, as well as details the underlying measurement principles for capacitive and passive EPS sensing. In this extended version, the focus shifted towards Sect. 4, where the toolkit is thoroughly evaluated. Besides the usage study, we present a deeper investigation into the performance evaluation, specifically stability issues of capacitive sensing on wirelessly connected, low-power devices. We identify a limit to the assumption of possible detection range often found in literature and finally present a variety of use cases as demonstrations which were realized since the toolkit's introduction. Section 5 concludes this paper.

2   Related Work

This section presents the result of a literature study on available toolkits in the HCI area of unobstrusive proximity mearsurement. We limit this section to only very closely related toolkits. The interested reader can be referred to the meta study of evaluations of HCI toolkits by Lado et al. [9].

The open-hardware Proximity Toolkit [11] provides interfaces for high-level proximity representation and visualization in proximity aware applications. It is a very general toolkit, interoperable with a variety of sensors. The focus is on interaction concepts, and specifically adapts the feedback for users to the dimensions for proximity in ubiquitous computing defined by Greenberg *et al.*, namely information on "orientation, distance, motion, identity and location information between entities" [5]. The toolkit is, similar to ours, motivated by the overhead of sensor data acquisition.

A toolkit to enrich ordinary objects with touch interaction is presented in [12]. As we aim for contactless interaction, the focus is slightly different, but interaction concepts and reception are interesting for this project.

CapToolkit by Wimmer et al. [16], and shown in Fig. 2a, is a toolkit in the area of capacitive sensing and an indirect precursor to this work. Up to eight loading mode sensors can be connected via USB at a sampling rate of 25 Hz to 100 Hz. It support dynamic run-time reconfiguration. CapToolkit has a detection range of up to 1 m for human bodies and 50 cm for hand movements (with a 10 cm × 10 cm electrode). The given claimed spacial resolution of 1 cm at 25 cm was not be reproduced by [6].

Successing the CapToolkit is the OpenCapSense board in Fig. 2b. It expands upon the CapToolkit in three ways. First, new sensor types supporting other capacitive modes, as well as EPS measurment [7] are introduced. Secondly the maximal sampling frequency is increased to 250 Hz with eight and up to 1 kHz with one sensor attached [6]. Lastly, an option to combine multiple toolkits into a sensor array devised. The number of sensor ports is identical to the CapToolkit.

The OpenCapSense has been well established in prototyping and research projects [1]. Compared to the Linoc toolkit, the modular sensor concept differs. Linoc has a stronger focus on usability and supports wireless connection types, enabling stand-alone IoT applications.

As we see, the Linoc toolkit neatly fits in line with its two closest predecessors. Besides benefiting from recent developments in mircoprocessor technology, it was also designed under different design goals.

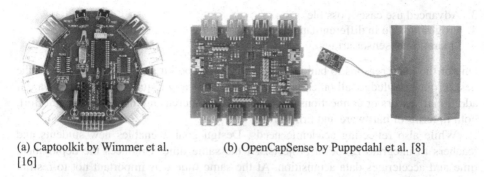

(a) Captoolkit by Wimmer et al. [16]   (b) OpenCapSense by Puppedahl et al. [8]

Fig. 2. Two examples of existing capacitive sensing toolkits: (a) Captoolkit and (b) Open-CapSense.

3 The Linoc Toolkit

This section presents the Linoc prototyping toolkit. Starting with the design goals, we motivate the need for a new toolkit and introduce quality criteria. Following we describe the most important hardware aspects, namely the deployed microcontroller, the connectivity possibilities, as well as its sensor groups. A brief overview of the firmware concludes this chapter. Figure 3 shows the final Linoc toolkit with its components.

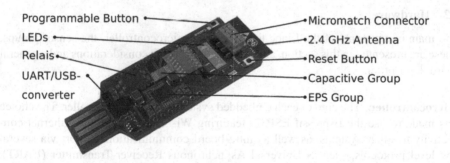

Programmable Button — Micromatch Connector
LEDs — 2.4 GHz Antenna
Relais — Reset Button
UART/USB-converter — Capacitive Group
— EPS Group

Fig. 3. The Linoc prototyping toolkit with highlighted and labeled connection methods, sensor groups and components for user interaction. Graphic from [15].

3.1 Design Goals

While creating the Linoc toolkit, we had several use cases in mind it had to cover and should be flexible enough to cover even more. That is why in the planning phase, the following design goals were identified:

1. High connectivity
2. Ease of use

3. Advanced use cases possible
4. Programmable in different languages
5. Operation in sensor arrays

One of the main reasons to build a new prototyping toolkit was Design goal 1. To the best of our knowledge, all other existing toolkits typically require external hardware if additional sensors or connections are required, thus increasing the development effort, both in terms of hardware and firmware.

While also reflecting academic needs, Design goal 2 enables new students and teachers to integrate Linoc in projects. At the same time it reduces the deployment time and accelerates data acquisition. At the same time it is important not to restrict experienced users by an unflexible framework, which is reflected by Design goal 3.

Linoc was designed so that it can be programmed in several languages as stated by goal 4. This empowers users to use the most familiar programming language and/or the one most fitting for the current project.

Finally, goal 5 reflects a lesson learned from working with other toolkits: there are always use cases in which you need more sensors than the toolkit has, no matter how many these are. Expeptions are, e.g., the OpenCapSense toolkit, which can be used as a sensor array, connected via CAN-bus. This however requires reprogramming and thus decreases the ease of use aspect. The combination of these two design goals allows an easy acquisition of higher dimensional data.

These design goals will now consecutively be applied to the toolkit's hard- and firmware.

3.2 Hardware

The main components of the Linoc toolkit are its microcontroller, the sensor groups. These are presented in this section, along with connectivity considerations and a general board description.

Microcontroller. The core of each embedded system is its microcontroller. The choice was made to use the Espressif ESP32, featuring Wi-Fi, Bluetooth and Ethernet connectivity to other systems, as well as intra-board communication support via several low level protocols, such as Universal Asynchronous Receiver-Transmitter (UART), Inter-Integrated Circuit (I^2C), Inter-IC Sound (I^2C), Controller Area Network (CAN bus) and Serial Peripheral Interface (SPI). As the ESP32's processor family is widely adapted in the maker-scene and in commercial Internet of Things (IoT) products, multiple toolchains and different programming languages such as Python, C, C++ and JavaScript can be used for development. Meanwhile, the ESP32 is powerful enough to support Real-Time Operating Systems (RTOSs), allowing complex use cases. Summarizing, the ESP32 satisfies the design goals 1, 4 and 3.

Capacitive Sensing. Two capacitive loading mode sensors are embedded directly on the Linoc toolkit, eliminating the need for external hardware. A 555 timer generates high-frequency, constant-current charging cycles, as shown in Fig. 4. With constant charging current, the charging time is only dependent on the environment.

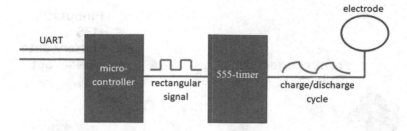

Fig. 4. Model of the capacitive sensor [13]. The microcontroller dis-/enables the 555 timer, which then generates charging cycles. The number of achieved cycles depend on capacitive objects in the proximity of the measurement electrode.

A moving conductive object in proximity of the sensor electrode influences the capacity between object and electrode: decreasing distance increases capacity and vice versa. The increase in capacity in turn increases the charging time. This underlying physical principle is operationalized as measurement concept, by counting the number of cycles per second. To prevent cross-talk between active sensors, the processor can en- and disable specific sensor groups. Furthermore the sensor groups are shielded. The shielding electrode is charged by a voltage follower circuit, following the capacitive feed line.

Electric Potential Sensing. In addition to the capacitive sensing groups, Linoc also features two passive EPS groups. EPS is a specialized form of capacitive sensing, with differences in operation mode, detection range and energy consumption. Moving conductive objects can be dectected up to ranges of two meters, whereas loading mode capacitive sensing is limited to about 35 cm. Instead of measuring capacity between electrode and a conductive object, glseps measures the induced current that a moving object induces in the virtual capacitor between electrode and object. Consequentially EPS is limited to moving objects in contrast to the loading mode sensor groups. A third difference is the energy consumption: EPS uses significanltly less energy, as the measurment is done passively and does not require charging cycles.

Board Layout. One of the striking features of the Linoc toolkit is the multitude of connection types as shown in Fig. 5. This is intentionally so, to be able to transfer measurement data through various connections and protocols, so that the data acquisition process is facilitated.

Three freely programmable Light-Emitting Diodes (LEDs), a programmable button and a reset button can be used for user interaction.

A mosfet relais enables users to connect more hardware, such as LEDs or piezo buzzers, in the range of up to 30 V and 1 A.

The micromatch connector can be used to connect multiple boards to a sensor array, via ribbon cables. Any number of Linoc boards, at any spacing can be connected that way. For easy reprogramming, the Linoc toolkit can be flashed via the front USB connector. An onboard USB to UART converter eliminates the need for an external programmer, common to many toolkits.

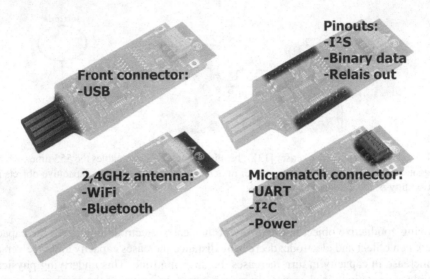

Fig. 5. Linoc's connectors and their functionalities as highlighted in the respective graphic.

3.3 Firmware

Following our design goals, we anticipate that only a minority of users will be required to write or modify the running Linoc firmware.

Therefore our Linoc firmware is build to enable dynamic reconfiguration of most toolkit features. A text console, accessible via UART, can be used to configure sensor groups, sampling frequency, start or stop Wi-Fi connectivity, set up sensor arrays, print a list of available options, and to print system diagnostics.

The firmware is written in C with the ESP-IDF toolchain and uses FreeRTOS operating system features. Advanced users, interested in modifying the firmware, are thus enabled to access low-level microcontroller functionalities, supporting design goal 3.

Multiple sensors can form a sensor array (design goal 5). The communication between boards happens via I^2C. After initiating the setup of the sensor array from the primary device (the one connected to the user's computer), the order of the array is established by the user, through pressing the programmable button on each connected Linoc in the intended order. Various physical setups are possible, the user only has to map the order to the data processing.

Sensor data is transferred to the host computer via UART, or via Transmission Control Protocol (TCP) through a Wi-Fi connection. Either data is posted from the toolkit to a configured external TCP server, or by running a TCP server on the toolkit, to which other devices can connect to. This data can then be processed by the user with her preferred tools or programming language. That way working prototypes can easily be build, without rewriting the toolkit's firmware.

4 Evaluation

In a meta-study by Lado et al. [9], evaluation strategies of 68 published toolkits are analyzed, and common pitfalls identified. From their evaluation categories, we chose to evaluate in terms of usability, performance and demonstration. Besides enabling better comparability to other toolkits, this approach best helps us to identify shortcomings in the design. The remainder of this section concerns with evaluation in these three categories, starting with a user evaluation to measure usability.

4.1 Usability

A set of tasks was devised to explore the functionality of the toolkit. The instructions on the tasks were vaguely formulated on purpose, in order to determine if the toolkit's interfaces are designed intuitively, and whether the information provided through the firmware console is sufficient. Advanced tasks were even only given as concepts to provide some freedom for the participants to explore the toolkit. The evaluation took place through a Likert scale questionnaire after completing the test procedure. The questionnaire is appended in Appendix A.

Eleven participants were included in the study, with varying levels of prior knowledge and technical background. After some time to familiarize with the toolkit and the way the commands work, most participants became more fluent over time. The participants needed about 20 to 30 min to complete the entire survey, explaining the small sample size.

The results of the questionnaire are presented in Table 1. Usage of the toolkit, and even the complex task of setting up a sensor array, were reported as intuitive. Even participants identifying as not experienced in programming or computer systems, mostly did not feel overwhelmed.

Eight out of the eleven participants reported receiving assistance during the study, mostly limited to occasional clarifications. Two minor technical problems occurred during the evaluation and consequently resulted in more assistance required to finish the tasks. Nearly all participants were able to complete all the given tasks successfully.

As the results of the evaluation in Table 1 shows, the overall feedback is very positive. Ideas for future toolkit applications of the toolkit centered around general activity and proximity detection, and integration to cloud computing.

4.2 Performance

To asses the performance of the capacitive sensor groups, an automated test stand from [10] was used, depicted in Fig. 6. The feature of interest is the resolution and achievable distance of the sensors, i.e., for which ranges it is possible to distinguish between two consecutive distances.

Automated Testing. The test procedure was devised as follows: The toolkit is mounted in the test stand and a three minute settling time is elapsed, to prevent remaining residual charges to effect sensor readings. Afterwards the sensor values are recorded for several

Table 1. Results from the questionnaire, ranging from 1 (strongly agree) to 5 (strongly disagree). These findings were originally reported in [15].

Question	Mean	Deviation
Experienced User? (technically)	1,91	1,6
Experience in similar systems?	3,09	1,51
Completed tasks successfully?	1,45	0,69
Feeling overwhelmed?	4,18	1,25
Usage intuitive?	1,82	1,25
Functionality sufficient?	1,09	0,42
Sensor-array setup intuitive?	1,82	0,98

minutes in the initial static state. Then the test bench's capacitor arm is moved upwards in 1 cm steps and held at this position for 100 s. The sensor integration time for pulses was set to 0.5 s, giving a 2 Hz output rate. Thus over 200 samples were recorded at every distance step of the test procedure.

The data from one of these test runs in depicted in Fig. 7. We use a graphical representation with error bars, to visualize which distances are distinguishable. The maximal possible range is the point where this is no longer possible. To decide if a distance is distinguishable from the previous the metric from Eq. (1) is used.

$$\bar{m}_i - \bar{m}_{(i-1)} - \sigma_i - \sigma_{i-1} > 0 \tag{1}$$

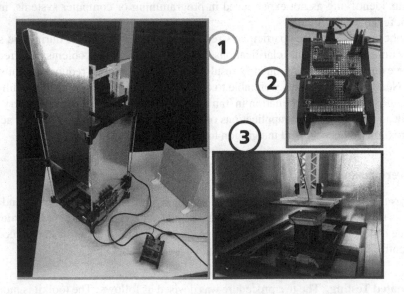

Fig. 6. 1) The "CapLiper" automated test environment from [10]. 2) External controller. 3) Grounded test platform positioned over test stand. Graphic from [10].

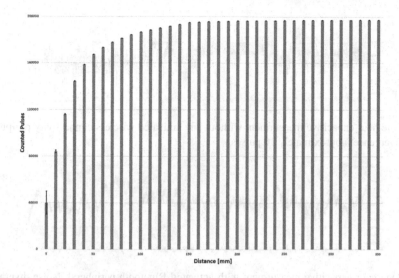

Fig. 7. Data of one test run in the automated test stand. For each measured distance, the number of counted pulses are plotted with the respective standard deviation. First published in [15].

If the mean value at a distance $\bar{m}_i$ minus its standard deviation σ_i, is bigger than the mean value of the previous measured distance $\bar{m}_{(i-1)}$ plus its standard deviation σ_{i-1}, all sensor values of these two distances can be clearly distinguished.

From repeated tests we derived at a maximum range of 35 cm in this shielded test setup. This matches the performance of the OpenCapSense toolkit.

Contrasting to prior literature [6], we found that the absolute achievable range with capacitive sensor does not scale infinitively with electrode size, but converges at approximately 30 cm. This finding could be a result of our automated test stand and estimated to be at a different range in other settings. One possible explanation is, that previous studies did not investigate sufficiently large ranges to reach the area of convergence. We found that larger electrodes show a significantly better detection resolution in the near field. This supports our hypothesis, as it increase the detectable range in the near field by providing better differentiation.

The large variance in Fig. 7 at a distance of 5 mm, is within the settling time of the sensor. This is why the first values of the loading mode sensor are noisier and are typically discarded.

Peripherals vs. Noise. While implementing the firmware for the microcontroller, we observed an increase in sensor noise as firmware complexity increased. Following factors made it difficult to assess signal quality at first:

- Capacitive measurements require a few minutes to tune in before producing a stable signal.
- The wide range of sensor value amplitudes make it difficult to make assessments based on numerical or graphical representation alone.

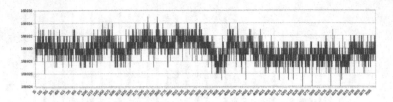

Fig. 8. One hour capacitive measurment without any activated wireless connectivity peripherals. Noise divergence: approximately 10 pulses.

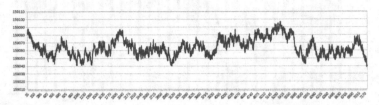

Fig. 9. One hour capacitive measurment with activated Bluetooth peripheral. Noise divergence: approximately 50 pulses.

- The absolute amplitude of the signal is dependent on various factors: environment, capacity of the object with which the change in capacity was induced (plus floor surface and shoe materials if charge is induced by a person), as well as electrode size, and the connection between host computer and Linoc board.

These factors were the initial reason to employ an automated test procedure. Different firmware versions, with different activated microcontroller peripherals were compared this way. The automated test setup is discussed in Sect. 4.2.

The different behavior of firmware versions is shown in Fig. 8 and Fig. 9. Both recordings of a single capacitive sensor were measured for an hour. In this period, the sensor was placed in a shielded environment, so the ideal result would be a relatively flat curve, measuring only environmental noise. Even though the same sensor was used in both tests, the measurement with activated Bluetooth radio shows a five time larger divergence than the sample without.

To further investigate this behaviour, several firmware version were compared to each other. Figure 10 shows a graphical comparison of six different firmware versions. The features of these version differ in several points;

- "Version 1.0": This firmware version is the first working sensor, based on reference implementations and examples provided by the microcontroller documentation. It used software tasks to query the pulse-counter unit of the microcontroller. Scheduling effects and delays however lead to imprecision of the exact duration after which the pulse-counter register is read out, leading to a higher or lower number of counted pulses. This explains why this firmware version performs underwhelmingly, despite its low complexity and few active peripherals.
- "Console": An implementation that eliminates the scheduling (context switching and processor load) issues. This was partially achived by executing time critical

code in timer interrupt handlers. Adittionally a console using the UART peripheral for user interaction was implemented.

- "Wi-Fi": An alteration of the "Console" firmware version with activated Wi-Fi radio.
- "BLE": In this firmware version, Bluetooth Low Energy was used instead of Wi-Fi. Note that the underlying peripheral for both, Wi-Fi and BLE, is the same 2.4 GHz radio. The difference in performance is explained by the different protocol. Shorter packet frames and less overall traffic in Bluetooth Low Energy cause less disruptions to the measurement.
- "Wi-Fi (stabilized)": The same firmware version as "Wi-Fi", but a 15 F super-capacitor is added to the Linoc board, functioning as a bypass capacitor to stabilized power supply and to provide high currents for short amount of times.
- "Chained": A chained sensor array setup consisting of two Linoc boards, in which the primary sensor uses Wi-Fi to transmit data recorded by the second sensor. The primary sensor is placed outside the shielded environment to enable wireless communication with the host. The intra-board communication was implemented via I^2C bus protocol.

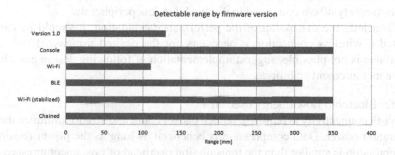

Fig. 10. Maximum measurement range of different firmware versions.

As shown in Fig. 10, the first implementation of the firmware "Version 1.0" achieved a limited range of 130 cm. This low performance can be explained with the implementation facts stated above. The firmware version "Wi-Fi" has a similarly low measurement performance, despite the fact that the implementation issues originated from the "Version 1.0" implementation were resolved. The reason for this are temporary power supply disruptions, even though large buffering capacitors are present on the Linoc board. To send a packet over radio, a large amount of power is needed in a short amount of time, resulting in a reduced supply voltage for the transimssion time. Altering the power supply voltage leads to a slightly increased or decreased amplitude of the generated charge/discharge cycles as shown by Fig. 4. To confirm this hypothesis, the toolkit was equipped with a 15 F super-capacitor, as depicted in Fig. 11. Our results, as presented in Fig. 10 show a significant increase in detection range with activated radio while the super-capacitor is present.

This also explains why the firmware is able to achieve better detection range when using Bluetooth Low Energy in contrast to Wi-Fi. BLE is designed to use less energy

Fig. 11. Toolkit equipped with a 15F super-capacitor.

and hence the fluctuations of the power supply are smaller compared to the "Wi-Fi" version. However it still degrades power stability, as observable performance reduced by approximately 40 cm compared to disabled wireless peripherals.

To conclude the discussion of the performance evaluation, it should be carefully evaluated if wireless connection is necessary for the desired use-case. If wired data transmission is not possible, suggest implementation of following design guidelines to improve measurement stability:

- Prefer Bluetooth Low Energy over Wi-Fi.
- If Wi-Fi connectivity is required, reduce packet count and size to minimize the radio operation power. Data compression is beneficial as long as the power required for compression is smaller than the transmission overhead of raw, uncompressed data.
- If the physical available space for the sensor is not constrained by its application, add additionally stabilizing capacitors to support a stable power supply.
- Alternatively, two chained Linoc boards can be used, to separate transmission from data acquisition. As shown in Fig. 10, firmware version "Chained" achievable range is significantly increased.

4.3 Demonstration

In this section, we will cover selected applications built with the Linoc toolkit. The purpose of this section is foremost to demonstrate the variety of applications that can be built with this prototyping toolkit, and not to detail each application in depth.

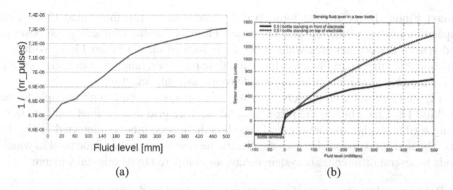

(a)   (b)

Fig. 12. Comparison of (a) the replicated fluid level metering and (b) the model in [16] ("sensor reading (units)" is plotted over "Fluid Level [mm]"). Note that the y-axis unit differs from the usual unit throughout this paper. Wimmer et al. measure the time of the capacitive charging cycles, and not the frequency. The relationship is $t = 1/f$ and the absolute value determined by the sampling length. This comparison was first published in [15].

(a) Person on a Smart Floor which is built with a wire grid connected to Linoc toolkits.

(b) Chained Linoc toolkits, placed on the edge of the Smart Floor wire grid.

Fig. 13. (a) A hidden capacitive sensor grid is used for fall detection in a living area. (b) The toolkit is deployed in a daisy-chained sensor setup to cover a larger area.

A ten Minute Built of a Fluid Level Metering. Wimmer et al. [16] used a fluid level metering to demonstrate the performance of their CapToolkit using a 10 cm × 10 cm electrode.

For comparison purpose we tried to replicate this demonstration. We noticed that after changing the fluid level, the signal took a while before stabilizing. The measurement was then performed in the stable region to prevent observer influence. Increasing the fluid level at 4 cl at a time we obtained a calibration curve similar to the one presented in [16]. Figure 12 shows both curves side-by-side.

Smart Floor. In its original form, built by Braun et al. [2], this Smart Floor used capacitive loading mode sensors. The Smart Floor is capable of tracking the position and size of the contact area while a person is located on the Smart Floor. With this functionallity, the Smart Floor can fulfill multiple purposes, ranging from energy saving or location based reminders to burglary detection and fall detection.

Figure 13 shows a newer version of the original system, built with multiple Linoc toolkits. The Linoc boards are placed around the wire grid in a chained configuration, using a ribbon cable to connect the Linoc boards to each other as depicted in Fig. 13 (b). The updated version also uses the electric field sensors of the Linoc toolkit, which leads to several differences in system behaviour compared to its original version:

– Better signal to noise ratio if a larger area is covered by the smart floor.
– It is harder to track non-moving persons since electric field sensing measures the displacement current induced by moving objects. Capacitive loading mode sensors are better able to detect non-moving objects.
– Electric field sensors are able to run at much higher sampling rates without sacrificing signal quality. Thus foster movements can be detected in more detail.

More details on Smart Floors based on electric field sensing were published by Fu et al. in 2017 [3] and 2019 [4].

Hidden Closet Switch. In this application, the Linoc toolkit is used to realize a simple switch, that triggers a voice application to report the current weather. This way, the user can be informed about weather conditions before opening the closet and choosing appropriate clothes. The hidden switch was placed at the upper half of the closet door to reduce false-positive trigger events.

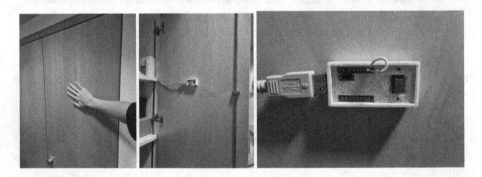

Fig. 14. Triggering the capacitive sensor which is placed on the inside of the closet.

Figure 14 shows how the weather report of the closet can be triggered by placing the hand onto the closet door. The illustration also shows the Linoc board installed at the backside of the closet door. The toolkit and the copper electrode are boxed in a 3D printed enclosure. To detect the hand in front of the door, a simple threshold detection in combination with the capacitive loading mode sensor group of the toolkit is used.

Person Counter. In this application, both electrical field sensors of the Linoc toolkit are used to implement a person counter, that registers entry and exit events of persons moving through a door. This is realized by designing the electrodes of both electric field sensors in such a way that they correspond stronger to persons moving on different sides of the door. The design is shown in Fig. 15. The electrodes are shielded in the middle of the sensor to direct each electrode to one direction. The outer shield was placed to filter various types of disturbances from regions not relevant to the sensor [14].

Fig. 15. Doorsensor

When walking through the door, each step of a person will cause a deflection of both sensors, but with different amplitudes, depending on which side of the door the person is moving. This is differentiated by an algorithm, calculating the differences of amplitudes of both sensors. With this information, the sensor can distinguish four different cases: a person moving inside the room, moving outside the room, entering the room or exiting the room. A more precise description of the design of the physical sensor and the algorithm used is given in our original publication"Improving Presence Detection For Smart Spaces" [14].

5 Conclusion

In this paper, we discussed the engineering goals and design process of the Linoc prototyping toolkit. Along the way, we also show how certain active peripherals of the microcontroller can influence sensor measurements, that require a very constant power supply. From this, we compiled guidelines on how to improve measurement stability in low-power, connected capacitive sensors boards. We showed that our proposed prototyping toolkit is able to measure objects up to a distance of 35 cm with its capacitive loading mode sensors. The electric field sensors are capable of significantly higher ranges, as shown in the application section of this paper, however a precise value for their range is difficult to obtain, since external factors play a much bigger role for this sensor type. Example implementations of our toolkit in various prototypes demonstrate the diversity of the Linoc prototyping platform. Although the board has a broad spectrum of applications, it is still easy to use, which was shown in our user study.

A   Questionaire

This questionnaire was used to evaluate the toolkit in terms of usability. It was first published in [15].

TECHNISCHE
UNIVERSITÄT
DARMSTADT

Evaluation of the Prototyping Platform for Capacitive and Electrical Field Sensing

1 Introduction

The Linoc toolkit is built for activity detection through electric field measurement and has two measurement techniques: capacitive and passive electric field sensing.

Its benefits are easy reconfiguration of sensor groups and connectivity without knowledge of embedded systems.

button for user interaction
connector for sensor array
pinouts for electrodes
USB connection
reset-button

2 Setup

The Linoc sensor is connected to the computer via USB. The electrodes are connected to the pin-outs at the side of the board. Labels are on the bottom side of the chip.

2.1 Connection Setup

To communicate with the sensor a couple of steps are necessary.

Windows:

In the device-manager it can be checked if the Linoc is detected correctly. If this is not the case, the right device driver has to be installed from www.ftdichip.com. The connection is then made with the program Putty (putty.org). After the installation, start Putty with the option serial, the com-port from the device-manager, a baud rate 115200 and without hard- and software control flows. Messages should now appear in the terminal.

Linux:

Start a terminal (Ctrl+Alt+t). The current user has to beeing to the group dialout
This can be checked with following command:
groups | grep 'dialout'
If the output is empty the user has to be added to the group using following command:
sudo usermod -aG dialout $USER
A reboot is necessary to apply the changes.

Linux & MacOS: Communication happens easiest via Putty.
(if Putty is not available it can be installed with 'sudo apt install putty'. Alternatives are screen, minicom, or other programs supporting serial connection). Putty is started with the option serial, the port (like /dev/ttyUSB0) and a baudrate of 115200

Messages should now appear in the terminal.

□ setup was completed successfully   □ setup was not necessary
□ messages from sensor are displayed   □ setup was not possible

1

Evaluation of the Prototyping Platform for Capacitive and Passive Electrical Field Sensing

2.2 Visualization (optional)

A graphical visualization helps understanding sensor values. A multitude of programs can be used for this. As example the Arduino IDE is mentioned here (https://www.arduino.cc/en/Main/Software). The respective port has to be selected in the menu 'Tools'. Afterwards the 'Serial Plotter' can be started from the same menu. The 'Serial Monitor' can be used to change the configuration.

Abbildung 1: Putty window. relevant settings marked with circles

2

Evaluation of the Prototyping Platform for Capacitive and Passive Electrical Field Sensing

3 Configuration

3.1 Console

The configuration of the Linoc toolkit happens over a console. The console can be reached through pressing the button on the board, on the side with the connector notch.
Typing help displays an overview of available commands.
□ Console is displayed   □ Commands are executed

3.2 Changing the Sensor Configuration

With the commands *capacitive_switch*, *eps_switch* and *frequency_set*, the sensor configuration can be changed. With *exit* the sensor returns to displaying values, *sensor_info* displays the current setup.
Please configure the sensor to the configurations described in the sections below and check if the values change if you move your hand towards the measuring electrode. For the configuration it might be necessary to change the placement of the electrodes on the chip.

3.2.1 Task 1: Configuration #1

Active sensors: Capacitive 1 & 2
Sampling frequency: 2 Hz
□ Two value pairs are printed per second

3.2.2 Task 2: Configuration #2

Active sensors: EPS 1
Sampling frequency: 50 Hz
□ Values appear noticeably faster

3.3 Task 3: Connect to Wi-Fi

Connect to the provided Wi-Fi hotspot and start a TCP server on the sensor.
Stop the connection again afterwards.   □ values can be queried from another device
□ connection established successfully.

4 Sensor Array

Multiple Linoc sensors can be connected to a sensor array (Daisy Chain).
The command to initiate is 'daisy_chain init'.
Follow the instructions provided in the console from now on.
The connected devices takes the role of the master and queries sensor values of the other sensors.

4.1 Task 4: Sensor Array Setup

Connect 3 sensors with the provided cable to a sensor array

4.2 Task 5: Configuration

Follow the instructions in the console to setup all sensors.
□ Number of sensors detected correctly   □ Sensor values of all sensors are printed correctly

4.3 Break up the Sensor Array

Stop the sensor array. This is done with the command 'daisy_chain break'.
Check if the sensor can be used as before.
□ Sensor array stopped   □ Sensor can be used as before

Evaluation of the Prototyping Platform for Capacitive and Passive Electrical Field Sensing

5 Evaluation

Please answer following questions briefly:
Age: __ Years
Gender: □ F   □ M   □ n.b.   □ n.A.
What is your current occupation: □ school   □ study   □ apprenticeship   □ work   □ something else

Which operating system are you using?   □ Windows   □ Mac   □ Linux   □ n.A.
Did you receive help with the tasks?:   □ Yes   □ No

Are you experienced in programming and/or computer systems?
strongly agree — agree — neutral — disagree — strongly disagree

Have you worked with similar toolkits?
strongly agree — agree — neutral — disagree — strongly disagree

Did you manage to fulfill the tasks with the information provided?
strongly agree — agree — neutral — disagree — strongly disagree

Did you at any time had the feeling to be overburdened?
strongly agree — agree — neutral — disagree — strongly disagree

Was the handling of the Linoc toolkit intuitive?
strongly agree — agree — neutral — disagree — strongly disagree

Do you think the functionality is sufficient?
strongly agree — agree — neutral — disagree — strongly disagree

Was the setup of the sensor array intuitive?
strongly agree — agree — neutral — disagree — strongly disagree

5.1 Free questions

What did you like about the system?

What did you dislike?

Could you imagine using the toolkit in a project?

Which applications can you imagine?

Which aspects should be improved?

What would facilitate the handling?

Further comments:

References

1. Braun, A.: Application and validation of capacitive proximity sensing systems in smart environments. J. Amb. Intell. Smart Environ. **7**(5), 693–694 (2015). https://doi.org/10.3233/AIS-150341
2. Braun, A., Heggen, H., Wichert, R.: CapFloor – a flexible capacitive indoor localization system. In: Chessa, S., Knauth, S. (eds.) EvAAL 2011. CCIS, vol. 309, pp. 26–35. Springer, Heidelberg (2012). https://doi.org/10.1007/978-3-642-33533-4_3
3. Fu, B., Kirchbuchner, F., von Wilmsdorff, J., Grosse-Puppendahl, T., Braun, A., Kuijper, A.: Indoor localization based on passive electric field sensing. In: Braun, A., Wichert, R., Maña, A. (eds.) AmI 2017. LNCS, vol. 10217, pp. 64–79. Springer, Cham (2017). https://doi.org/10.1007/978-3-319-56997-0_5
4. Fu, B., Kirchbuchner, F., von Wilmsdorff, J., Grosse-Puppendahl, T., Braun, A., Kuijper, A.: Performing indoor localization with electric potential sensing. J. Ambient. Intell. Humaniz. Comput. **10**(2), 731–746 (2018). https://doi.org/10.1007/s12652-018-0879-z
5. Greenberg, S.: Toolkits and interface creativity. Multimedia Tools Appl. **32**(2), 139–159 (2007). https://doi.org/10.1007/s11042-006-0062-y
6. Grosse-Puppendahl, T., Berghoefer, Y., Braun, A., Wimmer, R., Kuijper, A.: OpenCapSense: a rapid prototyping toolkit for pervasive interaction using capacitive sensing. In: 2013 IEEE International Conference on Pervasive Computing and Communications (PerCom), pp. 152–159. IEEE (2013). https://doi.org/10.1109/PerCom.2013.6526726
7. Grosse-Puppendahl, T.: Capacitive Sensing and Communication for Ubiquitous Interaction and Environmental Perception. Ph.D. thesis, Technische Universität Darmstadt (2015). http://tuprints.ulb.tu-darmstadt.de/4568/
8. Grosse-Puppendahl, T., Braun, A., Dellangnol, X.: Prototyping capacitive sensing applications with OpenCapSense. GetMobile: Mobile Comp. Comm. **20**(2), 16–21 (2016). https://doi.org/10.1145/3009808.3009814
9. Ledo, D., Houben, S., Vermeulen, J., Marquardt, N., Oehlberg, L., Greenberg, S.: Evaluation strategies for HCI toolkit research. In: Proceedings of the 2018 CHI Conference on Human Factors in Computing Systems - CHI 2018, pp. 1–17. ACM Press (2018). https://doi.org/10.1145/3173574.3173610
10. Majewski, M.: 3D-printed Electrodes for Electric Field Sensing Technologies. Master's thesis, Technische Universität Darmstadt, Hochschulstraße 1, 64289 Darmstadt, Germany (2017)
11. Marquardt, N., Diaz-Marino, R., Boring, S., Greenberg, S.: The proximity toolkit: prototyping proxemic interactions in ubiquitous computing ecologies. In: Proceedings of the 24th Annual ACM Symposium on User Interface Software and Technology - UIST 2011, p. 315. ACM Press (2012). https://doi.org/10.1145/2047196.2047238
12. Savage, V., Zhang, X., Hartmann, B.: Midas: fabricating custom capacitive touch sensors to prototype interactive objects. In: Proceedings of the 25th Annual ACM Symposium on User Interface Software and Technology - UIST 2012, p. 579. ACM Press (2012). https://doi.org/10.1145/2380116.2380189
13. Siegmund, D., et al.: A look at feet: recognizing tailgating via capacitive sensing. In: Distributed, Ambient and Pervasive Interactions. 5th International Conference, DAPI 2018. Pt.2: Technologies and Contexts, pp. 139–151 (2018)
14. von Wilmsdorff, J., Fu, B., Kirchbuchner, F.: Improving presence detection for smart spaces. In: Müller, F., Schnelle-Walka, D., Günther, S., Marky, K., Funk, M., Mühlhäuser, M. (eds.) Smart Objects 2019, in conjunction with EICS 2019, pp. 14–20, June 2019. http://tuprints.ulb.tu-darmstadt.de/8961/

15. von Wilmsdorff, J., Lenhart, M., Kirchbuchner, F., Kuijper, A.: Linoc: a prototyping platform for capacitive and passive electrical field sensing. In: SENSORNETS, pp. 49–58 (2021)
16. Wimmer, R., Kranz, M., Boring, S., Schmidt, A.: A capacitive sensing toolkit for pervasive activity detection and recognition. In: Proceedings of the Fifth IEEE International Conference on Pervasive Computing and Communications, pp. 171–180. PERCOM 2007, IEEE Computer Society, USA (2007). https://doi.org/10.1109/PERCOM.2007.1

Performance Evaluation of Embedded Time Series Indexes Using Bitmaps, Partitioning, and Trees

Nadir Ould-Khessal, Scott Fazackerley[ID], and Ramon Lawrence[✉][ID]

University of British Columbia, 3187 University Way, Kelowna, BC V1V 1V7, Canada
nkhessal@okanagan.bc.ca, {scott.fazackerley,ramon.lawrence}@ubc.ca

Abstract. Sensor devices collecting, storing, and processing data use index structures to improve query performance. Indexing approaches based on trees, hash and range partitioning, and space efficient summaries such as bitmap indexes have been proposed. The most efficient technique to use for a particular use case is often unknown, and there has been limited research comparing the different approaches to determine situations where each is the most effective. This work presents an experimental evaluation of the sequential binary index for time series (SBITS) versus tree and partition index structures. SBITS uses space-efficient bitmap indexes and sequential writes that results in significantly higher insert and query performance. It also has the ability to adapt the index structure to both the query requirements and data distribution.

Keywords: Embedded · Index · Partition · Tree · Bitmap

1 Introduction

Embedded sensor devices collect time series data for environmental, industrial, and health applications. Performing data processing on the data collection device requires efficient storage and querying of the sensed data. There have been several different indexing approaches, specifically for time series data, proposed for embedded devices. The approaches may be based on a tree data structure, partitioning the data using hash or range partitioning, or by producing space efficient summaries of the data using bitmap indexes or Bloom filters [3]. This work performs an evaluation of the different techniques in order for developers to understand the benefits and tradeoffs of the approaches.

Prior work presented the sequential binary index for time series (SBITS) [4] and a theoretical comparison with indexes such as B-trees [14], MicroHash [23], linear hashing [5], and PBFilter [22]. The unique features of SBITS include its adaptability to different query and data patterns, and the use of sequential writes allowing for improved efficiency and operation on raw flash memory.

The contribution of this work is a theoretical and experimental evaluation of SBITS with indexing implementations based on partitioning (MicroHash) and

© Springer Nature Switzerland AG 2022
A. Ahrens et al. (Eds.): SENSORNETS 2020/2021, CCIS 1674, pp. 125–151, 2022.
https://doi.org/10.1007/978-3-031-17718-7_7

B-trees using realistic data sets and use cases. The results demonstrate that the limited memory available on devices combined with the specific characteristics of flash memory require index structures that are distinctive from indexes for server-based systems. Indexing structures that favor sequential writes have the highest performance. SBITS demonstrates overall superior performance.

The organization of this paper is as follows. The paper begins with a background on embedded devices and time series data collected by these devices. An overview of approaches to indexing on flash and embedded devices is presented. Implementations of each distinctive approach are created from best techniques and evaluated for their performance. Extensive experimentation compares SBITS with indexing using trees and partitioning on different memory types and embedded hardware. The paper closes with future work and conclusions.

2   Background

2.1   Embedded Devices

The embedded devices considered in this work are the smallest devices with very limited memory and CPU. Examples include nodes in a sensor network, consumer electronics, personal activity trackers, sensor monitoring and industrial IoT devices. The work does not examine indexing on more powerful devices such as edge devices in a sensor network or smartphones. The devices evaluated have a specific and limited function in a bare-metal configuration without an operating system, focused on data sensing and collection.

The limited CPU and memory resources constrains the algorithms and approaches that can be used. The CPU may be 8-bit, 16-bit, or 32-bit with a clock speed between 16 MHz and 128 MHz. Growth in the embedded device market has been driven by IoT applications, with 8-bit adoption continuing to grow at a steady rate due to its simplicity and low cost [1]. SRAM is often the most limited resource with quantity between 4 KB and 128 KB. External storage is frequently required, and there are a variety of flash-based storage devices ranging from raw NAND and NOR flash chips to packaged products like SD cards.

An example device is the 8-bit Arduino MEGA 2560 which is based on the Microchip AVR® 8-Bit ATmega2560 Microcontroller[1] with a 16 MHz CPU and 8 KB SRAM. There are numerous hardware platforms and configurations that are frequently purpose-built for specific use cases. Given these hardware constraints, there is typically no operating system or memory management unit. Devices operate as a bare-metal single-threaded application (no parallelism) focused on functionality and longevity. Systems must minimize I/O operations and memory to limit energy usage while maintaining acceptable performance levels.

The flash memory storage devices used with embedded systems have several important properties. First, writes are more time-consuming than reads. Given

---

[1] https://www.microchip.com/en-us/product/ATmega2560.

this unbalanced read and write performance, algorithms will perform more reads in order to avoid costly writes. Bytes are organized into pages, which form the minimum writable unit [11]. Flash memory contains an erase-before-write constraint, requiring that a page must be fully erased before data can be written to it. This constraint prevents modification of data in place. With data addition or modification, the page must be first read from the device to a buffer, modified and then written back to a previously erased location. With each erase/write operation, a flash page suffers incremental degradation described as device wear, ultimately leading to the possibility of data corruption over time. In general, a single page within a flash memory cannot be individually erased and must be erased in blocks of pages. For general purpose I/O patterns, the management of live data mixed with pages to be erased presents a challenging problem. In order to erase a block of pages, live data must be moved to another location, requiring an additional mapping structure to maintain page mappings. Some special application memories, such as Dialog Semiconductor's DataFlash[2] serial NOR flash allow for data to be erased on the page level allowing for easier data management compared to other flash memories.

For packaged flash products like SD cards, the raw flash chips are hidden behind a page-level abstraction layer. The software refers to logical pages (i.e. pages of a file), and a flash translation layer (FTL) converts the logical page requests to physical addresses in storage. This translation serves several purposes. First, it allows the software to ignore physical storage characteristics on the device and perform logical page writes (and overwrites). This simplifies implementations. The FTL handles logical page overwrites by selecting a new physical page in storage and updating its page translation table. The FTL also ensures that pages are written evenly throughout storage to avoid excessive wear in specific areas of the memory. While an FTL can be run on an embedded processor utilizing raw memory, the overhead is too great for resource constrained devices in terms of memory and run-time overhead. If the embedded device is interacting with raw flash chips without the benefit of the FTL, then the algorithm must handle the writes, erases, and overall memory management internally.

2.2 Flash Indexing

Techniques for indexing on flash utilize the flash memory characteristics to optimize behavior when interacting with the flash storage. A survey [7] on flash memory indexing overviews the approaches used. The most common technique is to favor reads over writes, as writes are costly and wear the device. Many storage devices have higher performance for sequential writes compared to random writes. This is often related to how the FTL allocates and maps addresses. Algorithms that use sequential writing have higher performance. Solid-state drives (SSDs) have opportunities for parallelism by performing multiple read/write requests simultaneously. Most approaches designed for servers and SSDs are not

---

[2] https://www.dialog-semiconductor.com/products/memory/dataflash-spi-memory.

applicable for embedded devices due to the high memory consumption and parallel storage architecture. Deferring and parallelizing writes requires buffering modifications in memory, and embedded devices have limited memory to use.

2.3   Embedded Indexing

Embedded indexing has two key differences compared to indexing on servers. The first difference is the low amount of memory and CPU resources. Index algorithms must bound their memory consumption in order to execute in this environment. The second difference is that embedded devices have specific operational goals compared to more general indexing required for servers. For instance, an embedded device will have a specific data set it collects and does not generally have to respond to ad hoc or user-based queries. This restricted operational domain allows for optimizing and customizing index structures.

Time series are the most common data collected by an embedded device [16]. Time series data may be environmental data (temperature, humidity, etc.) or operational data for sensors connected to machinery or electronics. A time series data set consists of a set of records where each record has a timestamp and one or more data values collected at that timestamp. The timestamp in time series data is always increasing. We will refer to time series data as a *sequentially ordered data set*. Inserting data in sorted order has a major impact on the indexing structure used and the associated performance. Sequentially ordered data sets also occur in situations such as an auto-generated, integer keys.

Indexing a time series data set requires indexing both the timestamp (which is sequentially increasing) and the data values, which are not. The data values typically have a restricted domain as they are produced by sampling through a sensor. These sampled data values are often a 10-bit to 16-bit integer before they are converted into a floating-point value.

Figure 1 contains an example time series data set used to describe the index approaches. Each record contains a timestamp measured in seconds as the first field and a sensed integer value as the second field. The timestamp starts at 0 for illustration but would usually be a value in seconds since UTC. The range of the sensed data field is small (15 to 30), which is common for sensed data. The records are grouped into 6 data pages each with 4 records.

Discussion of the embedded index techniques uses consistent notation summarized in Table 1. The number of pages used to store data is denoted by D, and the number of index pages by I. The index pages may be expressed as percentage of the data size D to characterize the index overhead. The number of data records per page is N_d, and the number of index records per page is N_i. The size of the memory available to the index is M pages. The page read and write costs are denoted by R and W respectively. The following sections overview the embedded indexing approaches.

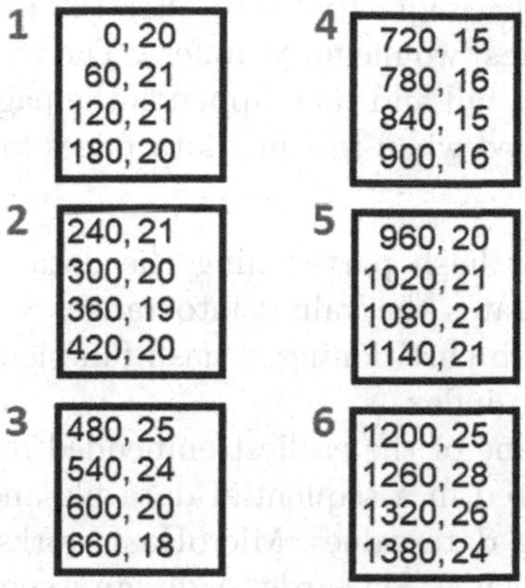

1	0, 20 60, 21 120, 21 180, 20	4	720, 15 780, 16 840, 15 900, 16
2	240, 21 300, 20 360, 19 420, 20	5	960, 20 1020, 21 1080, 21 1140, 21
3	480, 25 540, 24 600, 20 660, 18	6	1200, 25 1260, 28 1320, 26 1380, 24

Fig. 1. Example time series data.

Table 1. Index parameters.

Notation	Definition
D	Data size in pages
I	Index size in pages
N_d	Number of data records per page
N_i	Number of index records per page
M	Memory pages for use by index
R	Page read operation cost
W	Page write operation cost
s	Query selectivity

Sequential File. The simplest data indexing method is a sequential file. Each time series record is appended to the end of the sequential file as it is received. Buffering a page of records before appending to the file improves performance.

The advantage of a sequential file is its simplicity. Appending data is very efficient and requires no data overwriting. Since the data is collected in sequential order by timestamp, the sequential file is sorted by timestamp. Queries on timestamp can be performed in $O(logD)$ using binary search. There are no index pages and no index overhead. Recovery is simple as there is no data overwriting. It is also straightforward to delete old data by removing data from the start of the file. A sequential index structure was implemented in the embedded database Antelope [18]. The disadvantage of sequential files is that searches on data value are $O(D)$ and require a scan of the entire data file. Depending on the frequency of queries and the size of the data set, this is a major performance issue. Many data logging devices use sequential files due to their simplicity and portability. If the device performs only logging and timestamp queries and no query processing involving data values, then sequential files offer the highest performance. The sequential data file requires two memory buffers. The write buffer buffers records in memory until a page is full and then appends the page to the end of the data file. The read buffer is used when reading data pages for queries.

Partitioning. Range or hash partitioning the data allows for faster search. Range partitioning separates the values into ranges with each range having a bucket for storage. In hash partitioning, a hash function is computed on a value to determine its partition index.

MicroHash [23] was one of the earliest embedded indexing approaches. The time series data was stored in a sequential data file and an index built on top of it to allow for querying data values. MicroHash works with raw flash memory or storage with a FTL such as SD cards. A design issue is that data pages were intermixed in the sequential file with index pages with the goal of providing uniform memory wear. Unfortunately, intermixing data and index pages complicates time series searches. Although various modifications were proposed, the performance is slower than binary search.

A partitioning index allows for querying on data values. Despite the name MicroHash, the index was built using range partitioning (not hash partitioning). The domain of the data value was divided into ranges that could be further subdivided if the number of values in a partition grew beyond given bounds. When a record with a given data value was in a partition, the page number of the record was stored in the partition to allow for fast retrieval.

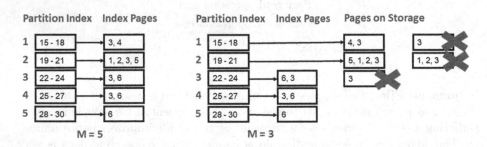

Fig. 2. Range partitioning example.

The performance of partitioning depends on the number of partitions and the memory available. Figure 2 shows the partitioning of the example data set into 5 partitions for two memory sizes $M = 3$ and $M = 5$. In the $M = 5$ case, each partition has a buffer in memory. The partition index contains the ranges of each partition and a pointer to the first page of each partition. Within an index page, there is a page id record if the page contains at least one data value in that range. For example, partition index 2 has index records to pages 1, 2, 3, and 5 as all have a value in the range 19 to 21. With a buffer for each partition, one page per partition index remains in memory and is only written to storage when completely full.

The $M = 3$ case illustrates the challenges with range partitioning. At most 3 index pages can be memory resident at a time. When an index page is not currently in memory, the system must write an index page to storage to free space. When processing data page 1, its data values are all in partition index 2. A buffer page is used for partition index 2 and the page id 1 is added to the index page. When data page 2 is written, its values also are all in partition 2, so page id 2 is added to the index page. For data page 3, a buffer is added for partition 1 and page id 3 inserted into the partition index. Page id 3 is also added to partition index 2 and 3. Page 3 also must be added to partition index 4, but there is no memory available. The index page for partition 1 is written to storage to provide space. Note that this index page has only one entry and has very poor space utilization. Data page 4 requires partition 1, which is no longer in memory. Partition index 2 is written to storage. The page for partition 1 is read into memory and the entry for page 4 is added. The previous page for partition 1 on storage is obsolete. Data page 5 requires partition 2, so partition index 3 is written to storage. The page for partition 2 is read from storage and updated. Finally, data page 6 requires partition index 3 and 4 so partition indexes 1 and 2 are written to storage.

A query for a given data value only must retrieve the pages that are in the same partition as the data value. For example, if the query was for all records with data value 15, then only partition 1 needs to be read which has data pages 3 and 4. Consider a data file with 1000 data pages. Each partition record is a 4 byte integer page id, so we will assume $N_i = 62$ records per 512 byte page. At minimum, the index size I is 16 pages if each page falls into only one partition. It is common that a page may have data values in multiple partitions so the page id would be inserted in each partition that it has a value in. Assume that 5 partitions are used. Then, to query for all records with data value 15, partition 1 is read. Assuming data is uniformly distributed, partition 1 would have about 3 pages of index and have page ids for 20% of data pages. Querying for all records with value 15 requires about 3 index page reads plus 200 data page reads.

The fundamental issue with partition based indexing is that the query performance depends on the number of partitions. With uniform data and D pages with P partitions, a query will read D/P data pages. Increasing query performance requires increasing the number of partitions. However, each partition requires a buffer in memory, and an embedded device is severely limited on memory.

MicroHash attempts to handle this issue by allowing more partitions than available memory buffers. This results in having to write out index pages that are not full whenever a buffer is needed for an index page not currently in memory. Although techniques are presented to limit the issue of partially full index pages, the fundamental issue is always present. The effect is mitigated to a degree when data values are slowly changing (e.g. temperature) making the partitioning more linear rather than random. However, the example demonstrates how the index utilization and performance drops dramatically if there are not enough memory buffers for each partition and a data page has values that span multiple partitions. It is possible to write multiple index pages for each data page written resulting in very low utilization and high query overhead.

Hash partitioning has less application than range partitioning as it will distribute values randomly across the partitions and does not support range queries that are common for embedded applications. Linear hashing has been implemented for embedded systems [5], although the implementation is not optimized for time series data and does not support range queries.

Our partitioning implementation based on MicroHash uses range partitioning with P partitions with the number of partitions and the ranges controllable by the index user. When defining an index, a partitioning function is supplied, written in C, that defines how to find a partition index for each data value indexed. The default partitioning function equally divides the range of data values into equal sized partitions.

The partitioning index is given $M - 2$ buffers (min. 1) with the other two buffers used for the sequential data file. If the number of partitions P is larger than $M - 2$, the algorithm ensures that when a partition is needed it is in an in-memory buffer. If a partition in memory must be evicted to free up space, the partition buffer is written to its partition index if changes have been made. When the partition buffer is required again, it is read from storage and updated.

A summary of the partitioning algorithm is in Fig. 3. Whenever a data page is appended to the data file, the partition index is updated. First, the data page is sorted on data value. Then, the records are scanned in sorted order, and for each data value its partition is determined. If the partition for a data value is the same as the previous record, no updates are performed. Otherwise, the page number of the data file is inserted into the proper partition. This repeats until all records in the page are processed. Note that a given page id may be in multiple partitions if it has data values that fall in multiple partitions.

```
write data page to sequential data file
sort data page in memory buffer by data value
for each record r in data page:
    if r is in different partition p than previous record:
        if partition p is not in memory:
            if no buffer space available:
                write out buffer for another partition
            read current page for partition p into buffer
        add record to partition with data page number
```

Fig. 3. Partition algorithm implementation.

For data queries, the partition(s) of the data values are determined. Each partition is scanned one page at a time. An index page is read into memory that contains page ids with values in that partition. Each data page is then read and values output. The partitioning implementation uses the best features of Micro-Hash with several optimizations. The key difference is the separation of data and index pages that allows for faster timestamp queries. Another optimization is building the index after writing each data page and sorting the records before determining partitions.

Trees. The B-tree has $O(logD)$ insert and query performance but performs random reads and writes. There have been numerous adaptations of B-trees for flash memory. Optimizations delay writes by buffering modified nodes in memory and using log-based approaches to log changes to the tree structure rather than immediately updating. Buffering techniques include write-optimized trees [2] that divide each page into a record area and a modification area. When the modification area is full, updates are pushed down to lower nodes in the tree.

Approaches based on logging rely on logging modifications in either a separate area of flash or on each page itself. One of the earliest flash B-tree implementations [19] used a log area that stores changes to the tree. When the log area was full, changes to the tree were performed in batch. The approach requires sufficient memory to buffer the changes in the log as well as a translation table for mapping pages to physical addresses. Log-structured merge trees (LSM-trees) [13] consist of multiple levels of B-trees with the top-level buffered in memory. LSM-tree variants offer high write performance with a trade-off of lower read performance and a large amount of memory consumed. The Always Sequential B-tree [15] uses buffering and writes updated pages sequentially to the end of the file. This avoids random writes but requires a logical mapping table as pages referencing an updated page are not updated themselves.

B-tree implementations for flash memory and SSDs are not executable on memory-constrained embedded devices if they do not adapt to the low memory available. Techniques based on buffering and deferred writes have limitations due to the limited memory that is available for buffering.

Some B-tree implementations work on raw flash memory without a FTL. The In-Page Logging (IPL) technique [12] uses logging areas associated with each page co-located on the same block. Using the logging area reduces the writes but requires more reads and a periodic merge process combining the log area into the tree structure. The Log-structured B-tree (LSB-tree) [9] used a log node for each leaf page and a mapping table to handle mapping leaf nodes to log pages. A B-tree implementation [14] for embedded devices that uses limited memory is available. For certain memory types, it may be possible to perform partial page flash updates in restricted cases [8].

B-trees are an efficient general index structure, however they are not specifically optimized for time series data. A single B-tree cannot index both the timestamp in the time series and the associated data values. Possibilities include using two B-trees, one for the timestamps as a primary index and one for the data values as a secondary index, or to use a sequential data file storing the ordered timestamp records that is indexed on data value using a B-tree. The B-tree indexing data values must be capable of handle duplicates.

Figure 4 contains a B-tree indexing on timestamp. Each leaf node is a data block that is ordered on timestamp. Each interior node provides key values for navigating efficiently to a data block. In this case, a leaf data block contains up to 4 records, and each interior node contains up to 2 keys. In practice, the number of keys in an interior node will be high. For example, with a 512 byte page and 4 byte key, each interior record (key and pointer) is 8 bytes and about 62 key/pointer pairs are stored in each page. This results in the height of the B-tree being small and any data page can be found in about 3 to 4 page reads.

Since the data is sorted by timestamp, building the B-tree index on times-tamp is very efficient and is similar to bulk index loading where the data is sorted before adding to the index. In this case, each data block written to the data file is always completely full. An index entry is added to the node above the leaf level. Each index node is filled completely before adding a new index node. This results in index utilization near 100% and no reads to insert a page of records into the index. Optimizing for sequential, sorted data in an index has been used in various databases such as PostgreSQL.

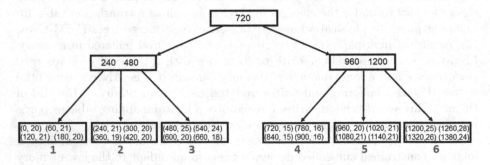

Fig. 4. B-tree primary index on timestamp.

Figure 5 shows a secondary B-tree indexing on data value that refers to the primary index. Each index entry is a tuple consisting of the data value and the page where it is present. This resolves the duplicate value issues in the B-tree. This index allows fast query by value to determine the pages where a given data value occurs. The index adds one entry per page even if a record occurs multiple

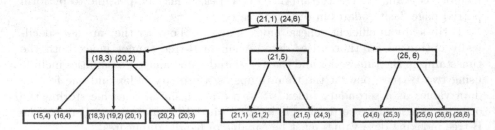

Fig. 5. B-tree secondary index on data value.

times. Since page level I/O is performed, there is limited benefit to indexing each record individually and indexing by page results in a smaller index size.

Two distinct B-tree implementations are evaluated. The first implementation is a sequential B-tree (sbtree) optimized for ordered data. The sequential B-tree implementation can be used instead of a sequential data file for storing the records sorted by timestamp. When inserting records, the sequential B-tree fills leaf and interior nodes completely full and requires no reads to find the page to insert the record. The sequential B-tree has slightly more index overhead than a sequential file, but also guarantees $O(log_{N_i} D)$ search performance. This is improvement over binary search as the number of index records per page (N_i) is often between 50 and 100.

A general B-tree implementation indexes the data values based on the B-tree implementation in [14]. The implementation handles duplicate data values by requiring that each key inserted into the tree consists of the pair (data value, page id) as shown in Fig. 5. An insert operation requires searching for the leaf page to insert the record into and then inserting the record. A record insert will modify the page which is overwritten if file-based storage is used with flash memory that has a FTL (such as a SD card). If no FTL is available and the memory does not support overwriting, then the modified page is written to the next sequential page in memory and a mapping is added in a mapping table that converts old page address to new page address. By using the mapping table, a page modification does not require updating other nodes in the tree with pointers to the page that was modified.

Similar to the partitioning implementation, when a data page is written to storage, the B-tree index is updated. The records in the data page are sorted, and B-tree records are added for each distinct data value in the page. Another variant was produced that added an index record for each data record in the page. This variant results in a larger secondary index size but allows for answering data queries without reading the data file itself.

The B-tree consumes one memory page for a write buffer. It also requires at least one page for a read buffer. Additional memory buffers supplied are used to cache recently used pages. Given sufficient memory, the root node of the B-tree is always cached.

When searching the time series by data value, the B-tree is used to find the leaf node containing the data value. Since a data value may occur in multiple pages, a scan of the B-tree leaf nodes is performed to retrieve all the page ids that contain the data value. The pages will be returned in sequential order as the B-tree sorts records by data value and page id.

Bitmaps. Bitmap indexes are common in data warehousing applications when indexing attributes with low cardinality. With a bitmap index, each potential attribute value is assigned a bit in a bitmap. When scanning the data set, only records (or pages) that have the corresponding bits set are read during the query. A bitmap index is memory efficient as long as the domain is small. There is research on encoding [21] and compression [17,20] methods for bitmap indexes.

PBFilter [22] used a sequential data file for storing data records that was indexed using a memory efficient key index. The key index consisted of Bloom filters. PBFilter wrote to both the data file and index file sequentially. By using Bloom filters, the index overhead was small and queries were efficient.

SBITS [4] is a sequential indexing scheme using a bitmap index. Both the data and index file are written to sequentially. Compared to PBFilter, SBITS consumes less memory and the index size is smaller. SBITS was designed for highly memory-constrained devices (4 KB to 128 KB RAM) and operation on either raw flash (NOR, NAND) or FTL-based storage (SD card). A unique contribution in SBITS was adapting the index directly to the embedded application. Given that embedded devices have highly constrained operational requirements, it is advantageous to modify the index for a specific use case and deployment.

The SBITS implementation buffers a page of records in memory and writes full pages sequentially to flash. When a page is written, a bitmap is added to the page header that summarizes the data values it contains. The size and construction of the bitmap is user-defined on index creation. The user supplies two functions: a bitmap check and a bitmap creation function. The bitmap check function takes a bitmap and a data value and returns true if the data value is in the bitmap. The bitmap creation function takes an existing bitmap and a new data value and updates the bitmap to include the new data value. SBITS allows any bitmap related filter including succinct range filters [24].

Figure 6 contains a bitmap index on the data value for the example time series. Instead of using a bit for each value in the domain (which is size 16 in the example data set), binning by ranges is used to assign a bit for each range. Using binning requires only 5 bitmaps. Customizing the binning and encoding strategy for the embedded use case can substantially improve performance.

The page bitmap is also written to an index file. For example using Fig. 6, when page 1 is written a bitmap of size 5 bits (01000) is written in the page header and to the index buffer. A page in the index buffer contains multiple bitmap index entries and the page id of the first page referenced by the first bitmap entry. When the index page buffer is full, it is written to the index file. The implementation requires one write buffer and one read buffer. After processing the 6 data pages, the index page contains 6 bitmaps of size 5 bits.

The default bitmap implementation uses bitmaps of size 64 bits and performs range binning uniformly in the data range. Given a page size of 512 bytes, each index page stores 62 entries with a 16 byte header. The index overhead is 1/64 or 1.6%. A 16 bit bitmap has overhead of 0.4%.

When performing a data query using the bitmap, the data range queried is mapped to a query bitmap. Only pages that overlap the query bitmap are read. For example, querying for the value 20 requires reading pages 1, 2, 3, and 5 as the bitmap B1 is set for those pages. Note that binning by ranges may result in false positives where the bitmap indicates a record in that range exists in the page, but it may not directly overlap with the query. For example, querying for the value 16 would read pages 3 and 4, but only page 4 actually has a value for

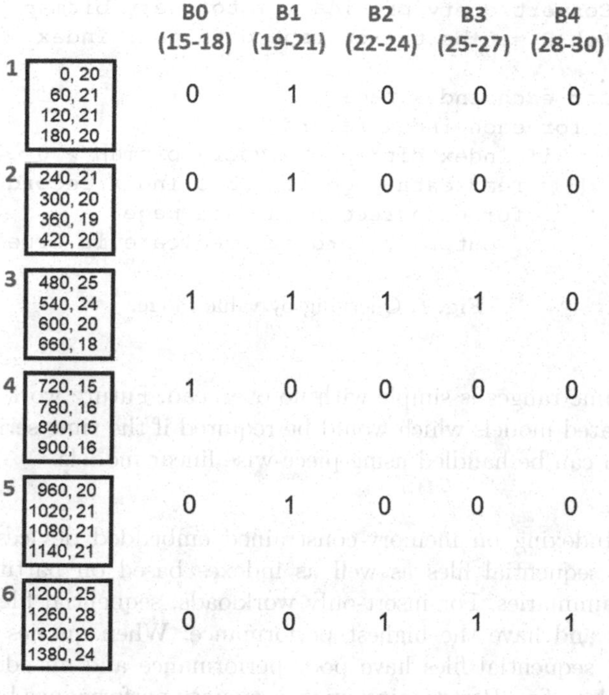

		B0 (15-18)	B1 (19-21)	B2 (22-24)	B3 (25-27)	B4 (28-30)
1	0, 20 60, 21 120, 21 180, 20	0	1	0	0	0
2	240, 21 300, 20 360, 19 420, 20	0	1	0	0	0
3	480, 25 540, 24 600, 20 660, 18	1	1	1	1	0
4	720, 15 780, 16 840, 15 900, 16	1	0	0	0	0
5	960, 20 1020, 21 1080, 21 1140, 21	0	1	0	0	0
6	1200, 25 1260, 28 1320, 26 1380, 24	0	0	1	1	1

Fig. 6. Bitmap index on time series data.

16. Querying a range of values, such as 20 to 25, requires processing multiple bitmaps (B1, B2, and B3), and reading a page if any bitmap has a 1.

The algorithm for a data query is in Fig. 7. SBITS reads each index page and processes each record. If the index record indicates a potential overlap of the data values with the query, then the data page is read and processed. SBITS will read all index pages and a number of data pages based on the query predicate selectivity s. The actual number of page reads depends on how the records matching the query predicate are distributed across the pages. If the query predicate exactly aligns with the bitmap vector such that no false positives are generated, then the algorithm will read the minimum number of data pages required and is optimal. A bitmap index can be constructed to support specific queries and get perfect matching with no false positives.

SBITS also implements an efficient timestamp search algorithm that is faster than binary search. The approach uses an interpolation search using a linear function that is determined based on the rate that records are inserted and the number of records per page. For applications with a constant record insert rate (e.g. every 60 s), it is possible to precisely predict the page location of a record based on its timestamp ($O(1)$). Variations of sampling frequency are handled by recording different linear functions for certain timestamp ranges. This approach has characteristics similar to learned indexes [6,10] that construct models to predict a record location in a sorted data set. Constructing the linear models

```
Convert query predicate into query bitmap
Let P = 0 be the current data page index

for each index page
  for each index record
    if index bitmap AND query bitmap > 0
      read data page for this index record
      for each record in data page
        output record if predicate is true
```

Fig. 7. Querying by value range.

for different time ranges is simple with no overhead. Future work may consider more complicated models which would be required if the time series show more variation than can be handled using piece-wise linear models.

Summary. Indexing on memory-constrained embedded devices can be performed using sequential files as well as indexes based on partitioning, trees, and bitmap summaries. For insert-only workloads, sequential files are efficient to implement and have the highest performance. When queries are added to the workload, sequential files have poor performance and an additional index structure has benefits. Partitioning improves query performance by dividing the records into partitions such that only partitions related to the query need to be read. Partitioning is limited by the available memory and performance decreases significantly if insufficient memory is available to buffer a page for each partition. Trees have consistent $O(logD)$ performance, but perform random reads and writes. Indexing the time series data values requires a B-tree to handle duplicates. If no FTL is available, the tree structure must also handle page overwrites and memory management. SBITS bitmap indexes are very space efficient, and the bitmap approach used is flexible to be optimized for particular use cases.

3   Theoretical Performance Analysis

Table 2 contains a summary of the theoretical space and query performance for the embedded index implementations. The following parameters were used with the model. The page size is 512 bytes. The key size is 4 bytes, and a page id (address) is 4 bytes. The bitmap index uses a 2 byte bitmap per page. Each page has a 12 byte header leaving 500 bytes of space for data or index records. For the analysis, the data distribution is assumed to be uniform, although performance will vary based on the data distribution in practice.

The sequential data file has no index overhead and requires the minimum amount of memory. Timestamp queries require a binary search on the data file, and data value queries require a scan of the entire data file.

Partitioning using P partitions requires $3 + P$ memory buffers, two for the sequential data file, one for reading partitions, and the rest for buffering a page

Table 2. Theoretical index performance.

Index	Index size	Buffers	Time query	Data query
Sequential data file	0	2	$log_2 D$	D
Partitioning	$0.008 * D$	$3 + P$	$log_2 D$	$D/P + 0.008 * D$
B-tree	$0.024 * D$	5	$log_{N_i} D$	$s * D + log_{N_i} D$
SBITS	$0.004 * D$	4	$O(1)$	$s * D + 0.004 * D$

per partition. Although it is possible to have less memory than this, the index size overhead and query performance will be negatively affected. Querying for a data value will read D/P pages with uniform data as well as the partition index pages. The minimum index overhead is 0.8% assuming completely full index pages, and each data page has values in only one partition. The index overhead could be an order of magnitude higher if these assumptions are not met.

The B-tree uses 5 memory buffers (2 for primary data file, 1 write buffer, and at minimum 2 read buffers). If a primary index B-tree is used on timestamp, the query performance is $log_{N_i} D$ as each index page contains N_i entries. N_i for the given parameters is 62, so the height of the tree is usually no more than 3 or 4. If using a secondary index B-tree and a sequential data file, then the timestamp query is $log_2 D$ (same as sequential file) and the data value query requires reading one page per height of tree (to find first leaf) then scanning other leaf nodes. s is the selectivity of the query. It is the number of data pages that contain values in the requested range. The minimum index overhead is 2.4% assuming B-tree index nodes are approximately 66% full.

The SBITS bitmap approach uses 4 memory buffers (2 for sequential data file, 1 write index buffer, and 1 read index buffer). Using the page location prediction algorithm of SBITS, the bitmap index can retrieve a given timestamp record usually in only one or two page reads. Its performance for data value queries requires scanning the index pages ($0.004 * D$) then reading any matching data pages based on the query selectivity (s). It is possible for the bitmap to produce false positives and read more than the minimum data pages depending on the bitmap binning and encoding technique used. The index overhead is 0.4%.

Overall, there are several key differences between the approaches. SBITS is the most space efficient, which results in fewer writes when building the index and reads when using it for queries. Partitioning may store a page id multiple times that occupies more space. The B-tree stores key and page id records that require at least double the space, and potentially more for larger key sizes. The performance of the B-tree for queries is consistent and may be the fastest for large data sets. However, its index overhead is the highest and requires many random reads and writes to maintain. Partitioning suffers from a fundamental issue of high memory consumption to buffer partitions that affects performance.

Table 3. Hardware performance characteristics.

	Reads (KB/s)		Writes (KB/s)		
	Seq	Random	Seq	Random	Write-read ratio
ATmega2560 (SD card)	200	200	125	50	1.6 (seq), 4.0 (rnd)
M0+ SAMD21 (SD card)	515	355	430	40	1.2 (seq), 8.9 (rnd)
M0+ SAMD21 (DataFlash)	475	475	38	38	12.5

4   Experimental Results

The two hardware platforms selected for these experiments are representative of hardware used in time series data collection sensors. The first platform uses an 8-bit AVR® ATmega2560 microcontroller with 256 KB of flash program memory. This platform was selected due to its small memory (8 KB of SRAM) and limited CPU performance (16 MHz clock speed). This is the processor found on the Arduino MEGA 2560 development platform and contains many common design elements found in applications. A SanDisk microSD card of 2 GB was used for storage attached with an Arduino Ethernet shield. The page size was 512 bytes. SD cards are typically used by developers for portability but also for convenience as they provide a block level interface to the storage using a built in FTL. Programs can use files on a SD card similar to other file systems.

The second hardware platform has a 32-bit Microchip ARM® Cortex® M0+ based SAMD21 processor with clock speed of 48 MHz, 256 KB of flash program memory and 32 KB of SRAM. The hardware board has several different memory types including a SD card and serial NOR DataFlash[3] which supports in-place page level erase-before-write. This platform was chosen as it represents devices with more capabilities and commonly used 32-bit ARM processors. Although the device has more memory and CPU power, it is cost-effective. Two memory types were selected for data storage, an SD card, that represents a typical use case for developers that want to simplify storage, and a raw NOR DataFlash to test performance on raw memory without a FTL. Summary of the performance characteristics of the hardware are in Table 3.

For the DataFlash if erase before write is not used (i.e. pages were pre-erased), write performance was 320 KB/sec. Read and write performance were measured by writing 1000 pages either randomly or sequentially and reading the pages either randomly or sequentially. Note the large difference for the SD card sequential versus random write performance. This difference is due both to the physical characteristics of the card as well as overhead of the FTL algorithm and the SDFat library used for accessing files. Performance on the DataFlash is consistent regardless if using sequential or random I/O. Reads are over 10 times faster on the DataFlash than writes.

The experimental data set was the real-world data set used in MicroHash [23]. This environmental data set consists of temperature, humidity, and wind

---

[3] https://www.dialog-semiconductor.com/products/memory/dataflash-spi-memory.

speed readings from various temperature stations in Washington[4]. The two stations used were located at the University of Washington (that sampled every minute) and at Sea-Tac airport (that sampled every hour). The timestamp was converted into a 4-byte integer representing a UNIX timestamp in seconds. The record size consisted of 16 bytes total including a 4-byte timestamp, 4-byte temperature, 4-byte pressure, and 4-byte wind speed. Indexing was performed on the temperature value.

All experiment results are the average of 3 runs. The memory allocated for the algorithms was determined by finding the minimum memory requirement that provided the best performance. The memory used was SBITS (bitmap) ($M = 4$), partitioning ($M = 5$), sbtree ($M = 3$), and btree ($M = 6$). On the ATmega2560 device, it was not possible to have large values of M due to the limited 8 KB of RAM and the SD card library using several KB of memory.

4.1 Insert Performance

Insert performance is critical as insert operations are the majority of operations performed by the embedded logging device. The one-minute sampling data was used, and the experiment evaluated inserting 100,000 records. The insert rate is shown in Fig. 8 for the ATmega2560 platform.

The sequential file has the highest performance. The SBITS bitmap approach is about 10% slower although it performs only about 2% more I/Os. The computation of the bitmaps and managing the index file takes time on the ATmega2560 as it has a slow clock speed. The sequential B-tree (sbtree) and partitioning approaches have roughly equivalent performance and about 30% less inserts/second. Both of these techniques perform no random writes or reads. The two B-tree implementations, one indexing per record and the other per page, have an order of magnitude slower performance due to the random reads and writes performed. It is important to note that even in this case, the inserts/second are 60 and 160 respectively on low-end hardware. This performance is more than adequate for devices that are sampling once a minute. All techniques have a stable insert rate even as the number of records inserted increases.

Additional data on the performance differences is in Table 4. This data includes the additional I/Os performed compared to the sequential file approach. The I/O numbers are independent of hardware. The data file size was 3226 pages for the 100,000 records. Percentages are given with respect to this size. Thus, a percentage of 102% for sbtree writes corresponds to 6504 writes (or double the amount required if storing just the data file itself).

The SBITS I/O results exactly match the theoretical values. The index size and additional writes represent an overhead of 1.6% compared to the data size. A 64-bit bitmap was used. The partitioning approach has good performance for the temperature data. The actual index overhead is 10%, which is higher than the theoretical minimum as data pages often have data values that fall into multiple partitions. The number of partitions was $P = 10$ with $M = 5$. Even though

---

[4] https://www-k12.atmos.washington.edu/k12/grayskies/.

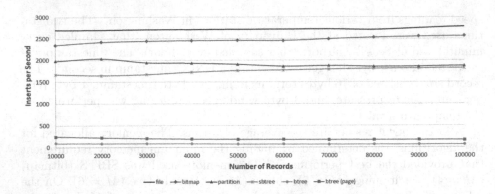

Fig. 8. Index insert performance on ATmega2560.

Table 4. Index I/O metrics for insert experiment - percentage additional I/Os compared to data file size.

Metric	SBITS (bitmap)	Partition	sbtree	btree	btree (page)
Reads	0%	0%	102%	102%	102%
Index reads	0%	9%	0%	7009%	1376%
Writes	0%	0%	102%	102%	102%
Index writes	1.6%	10%	0%	3293%	1204%
Index size	1.6%	10%	1.6%	98%	35%

there was not enough memory to buffer a page for each partition, overall the performance was still very good as the one-minute sampled temperature data changes slowly resulting in a data page typically only having values in one or two partitions. These results are consistent with the results for MicroHash [23].

The partitioning performance is fragile and highly depends on the data set. Using the temperature data set sampled every hour at Sea-Tac results in considerably different results. Each data page had data that was on average in 3.5 partitions. With $M = 5$, the algorithm was writing over 40 times more index pages with less than 2% index page utilization. To have similar performance as the one minute data set, $M = 11$ is required, which almost allocates one page buffer per partition ($M = 12$ allocates one buffer per partition with 10 partitions as the other two memory buffers are used for the data file). Although for certain use cases it is possible to have less memory available than partitions, in general this is not a stable situation.

The sequential B-tree has consistent, bounded performance and performs about double the number of writes compared to writing to the sequential file. The additional writes occur as the path from root to leaf is not buffered in memory. This results in at least one read and write of an index page whenever a completely full data page is written. The index overhead is 1.6% as the number of index pages is low. The sequential B-tree is only indexing the timestamps in the time series, not the data values, so its index performance is not directly comparable to the other approaches. The sequential B-tree performance is included to demonstrate the overhead of indexing only the timestamp using a B-tree structure and to provide some context with the B-tree indexing algorithm that uses a sequential B-tree to index the timestamps and a general B-tree for indexing the data values.

The insert performance of the two B-tree approaches (record-level and page-level indexing) is over an order of magnitude slower than the other approaches due to the high number of random reads and writes performed. Whenever a data page is written to storage, one or more index entries are inserted into the data value index. Each index record inserted writes at least one page and may write more if the B-tree index structure also requires updating. Unlike the sequential B-tree structure, these are random writes as the insert page could be any leaf node due to the data values not appearing in order. The page-level index approach only inserts a given (key, dataPageid) record once even if a key appears multiple times in the page. The record-level index approach inserts an index record for every data record. The page-level indexing approach has higher performance due to fewer records inserted into the data value index. It is also noteworthy that the index size is considerable relative to the data size.

The insert experiment was repeated on the 32-bit platform using both the SD card and DataFlash memory for storage. Figure 9 displays the insert performance on the DataFlash memory. The results are consistent with the results on the ATmega2560 platform. The number of I/Os are identical. The faster processor speed reduces the CPU overhead of the SBITS and partitioning methods that have relatively better performance compared to the sequential file. The B-tree performance remains significantly slower. Note that only the B-tree page level index is shown due to very high insert cost when indexing by record as shown in the previous experiment.

The absolute insert performance is slower for the DataFlash memory due to the cost of erasing before write. If the memory chip is pre-erased before inserts are performed, then the insert performance is three times higher. In general, the algorithm cannot be guaranteed that pages have been previously erased and must explicitly erase pages before writing. Unlike writing on a SD card, the algorithm must handle page erase, wear leveling, and ensure that it is managing memory directly as there is no FTL. In this raw memory environment, sequential algorithms like SBITS are easier and more efficient to implement as they write data pages sequentially. The B-tree with its random writes consumes significantly more memory pages and memory management is much more complicated.

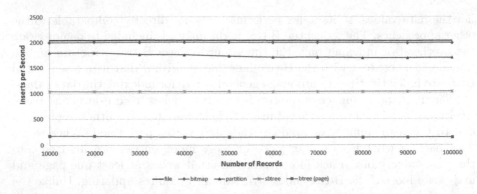

Fig. 9. Index insert performance on 32-bit platform using DataFlash memory.

The performance on the 32-bit platform using the SD card was consistent with the performance on the SD card on the ATmega2560. The absolute performance was about twice as fast as the ATmega2560 SD card and the DataFlash memory. Figure 10 presents the relative performance of each index method compared to using a sequential file on both platforms. The relative performance is presented as a reduction in insert rate compared to using a sequential file, so smaller numbers are better. On all platforms and memory types, SBITS is superior with no more than a 10% insert rate reduction. The partitioning approach varies between 15% and 30% rate reduction. The slightly higher variation is related to the partitioning approach having less relative performance loss for CPU intensive operations during the partitioning on the 32-bit platform compared to the 8-bit ATmega2560. The sequential B-tree insert rate is affected by its higher I/Os, and this is a larger factor on the faster 32-bit platform. The B-tree has an insert rate of less than 10% of a sequential file due to high I/Os.

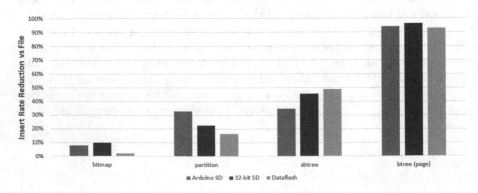

Fig. 10. Index insert performance compared to sequential file.

4.2   Timestamp Query Performance

Querying by timestamp is very common in time series data and is often used for timestamp range searches. Timestamp query performance was measured by performing 10,000 random timestamp queries on the data file containing 100,000 records produced during the insert experiment. The results are in Fig. 11.

Querying by timestamp on the sorted data file requires a binary search with about 11 page reads per query. The bitmap and partitioning techniques use the modified interpolation search algorithm of SBITS [4] that predicts the next page based on the data distribution. With the one minute data set, even though there are gaps in the data that make it not consistently one minute intervals, the algorithm is able to find the record in an average of 2.5 page reads. Note that the sorted data file could also use this approach in practice, and would be the recommended approach. Binary search was shown for comparison.

Both the B-tree and sequential B-tree perform a timestamp query using the same sequential B-tree index. The difference in performance is experimental variation. The query performance is very good, but slightly slower than using the interpolation search algorithm. An advantage of the B-tree approach is that the performance is consistent for all queries and requires 3 page reads with the first page read always the root that is buffered in memory.

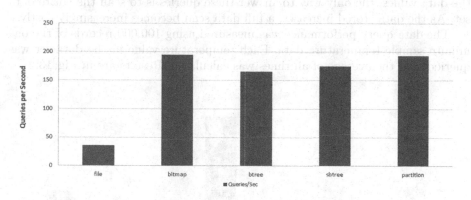

Fig. 11. Index timestamp query performance on ATmega2560.

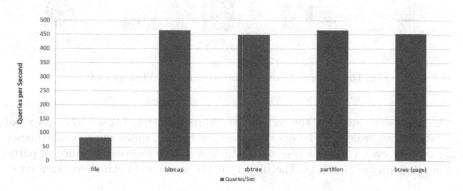

Fig. 12. Timestamp query performance on 32-bit platform with DataFlash memory.

It is important to highlight that the read performance is an order of magnitude slower than the insert performance seen previously despite writes being slower than reads for the storage hardware. Every query requires at least one page read to answer. In comparison, the inserts are buffered on a per page basis. A page is only written when full (31 records). This allows the insert performance to be higher than the query performance. For a use case where every record must be written to storage immediately after sampled (record-level consistency), the insert performance is considerably lower.

Figure 12 displays the timestamp query performance on the 32-bit platform on the DataFlash memory. Consistent with the results on the ATmega2560, the bitmap and partition approaches that use interpolation search are slightly faster than using the B-tree index for searching. The absolute query rate is higher on the faster hardware and memory, but the relative performance is similar due to the identical I/Os on both platforms.

4.3   Data Query Performance

Queries on the time series data values are used for aggregate calculations and to determine outliers. For the temperature data set, it is valuable to determine very low or high temperatures (e.g. temperature < 35). Without an index on the data values, the only way to answer these queries is to scan the entire data set. As the data stored increases, a full data scan becomes increasingly costly.

The data query performance was measured using 100,000 records of the one minute sample temperature data. Each temperature value in the data set was queried, and the average of all times was calculated. Results are in Fig. 13.

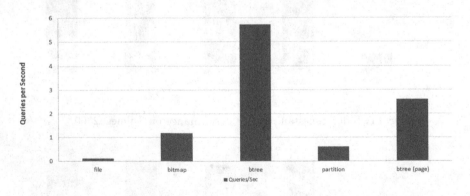

Fig. 13. Index data query performance on ATmega2560.

A data value query on the sequential file requires reading all 3226 pages of the data file regardless of the query value. The bitmap index query performance is on average over 1.2 queries/second, which is double the performance of partitioning (0.6 queries/second). The bitmap index is more selective requiring fewer data page reads. The partitioning approach is limited based on the number of partitions ($P = 10$), so with uniform data on average 10% of the data file is read for each temperature queried. However, the temperature data is not uniform with certain temperatures much more frequent than others. These results are consistent with results reported in MicroHash [23] where more data pages are read for frequent temperatures.

The fundamental issue with partitioning, as mentioned previously, is improving query performance requires increasing the number of partitions. Increasing the number of partitions is bounded by the limited memory, and insert performance dramatically degrades with too many partitions for the available memory. The bitmap approach allows for finer subdividing of the data set. Using the standard 64-bit range partition bitmap, allows for 64 distinct partitions and finer selectivity during queries.

The B-tree performance is very high, especially for the record-index version. The record-index B-tree can answer queries on data value entirely by using the index without reading the data file at all. The page-index B-tree requires reading the data page to get all values for a given temperature in that page. Overall, the cost of the inserts building the index pay off when performing queries on the index after it is built.

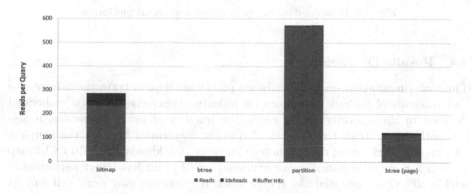

Fig. 14. Index data query I/O performance.

Figure 14 shows the I/O performance of the index approaches. The sequential file is not shown as it reads all data pages. SBITS reads all index pages (53 pages), and as many data pages as required based on the bitmaps. Compared to the partitioning approach, it reads more index pages but significantly fewer data pages. This is due to the partitioning approach only reading index pages for one of its partitions for each query. The partitioning is not as fine due to $P = 10$, which results in reading more data pages. The B-tree versions read fewer pages, with the record-index B-tree only requiring reading index pages.

The data value query experiment was repeated on the 32-bit platform for both the SD card and DataFlash memory. The data value query performance relative to the sequential file query performance is in Fig. 15. Higher values are better as the chart displays query rate improvement compared to the sequential file. SBITS has a query rate 10 times higher than the sequential file on all memory types and has the double the improvement compared to the partition method. A B-tree index has between 20 and 30 times query rate improvement. The relatively higher performance of the B-tree on DataFlash memory is partially due to the higher random read performance on the DataFlash.

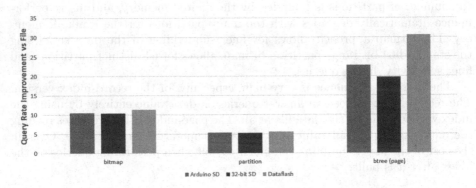

Fig. 15. Relative data query performance on all platforms.

4.4   Results Discussion

The experimentation on two hardware platforms demonstrate the advantages and tradeoffs of various techniques for indexing time series data on embedded devices. In the majority of use cases, the number of insert operations is significantly larger than the number of queries. Sequential files are the simplest and highest performing data structure for insert workloads. The SBITS bitmap approach requires minimal space overhead (<2%) and has insert performance within 10% of a sequential file. Range based partitioning may work well, but its performance is highly dependent on the data set and the range of data values in a page. For slowly changing data, the performance is good, but rapidly degrades if there is not enough memory to buffer a page per partition. Given that SBITS has higher insert performance and stability for all data sets, it is the better choice over range partitioning. B-tree variants have low insert performance due to the high number of random reads and writes. However, the performance, even on low-end hardware, is still sufficient to support tens of samples per second.

Queries on timestamp can be answered either using binary search on the data file, interpolation search, or using a sequential B-tree. For regularly sampled time series data, the performance of predicting the page location based on known sampling frequency and record sizes using interpolation is efficient to implement and significantly outperforms binary search. Interpolation search can be used instead of binary search for sequential files, bitmap, or partition indexes. Data sets with more variability could use more sophisticated models as developed for learned indexes [6, 10]. Using a sequential B-tree to index the time series data has consistent query performance with minimal overhead. Although slightly slower for large data sets, its consistent performance would be valuable in cases where sampling is infrequent and it is difficult to accurately determine a record location using this data.

If the use case requires any queries on the time series data value, an index on the data value has major benefits. Even though a sequential file has fast insert performance, executing one query requires reading all the data values and would significantly weaken overall system performance. SBITS has 10 times the query performance with only a 10% reduction in insert performance. It represents the best compromise between insert and queries for workloads with moderate query loads. SBITS dominates the partitioning approach for query performance. B-trees offer superior query performance and are recommended when the number of queries is very high relative to the number of inserts.

5   Conclusions and Future Work

The ability to efficiently store and query time series data is critical for embedded sensor devices. This work provides an experimental evaluation of bitmap indexing with SBITS compared to trees and partitioning to highlight the benefits and illustrate the issues associated with each approach. Although the dominant workload of embedded sensors is data logging (inserts), applications that use queries have improved performance when data values are indexed. Overall, using SBITS for a data index provides significantly higher query performance than sequential files with limited reduction in insert performance. SBITS represents the best performance trade-off for the majority of embedded query workloads.

Future work will deploy the indexing algorithms on a variety of platforms for environmental monitoring applications. Further experimentation is possible on different hardware types and memory configurations. The libraries for the indexing approaches are on GitHub.

Acknowledgment. The authors would like to thank NSERC for supporting this research.

References

1. Global Microcontroller Market Share, Industry Size, Application (Automotive Industry, Consumer Devices, and Industrial Sector), by Type (8 bit, 32 bit and 16 bit), 2021 By Radiant Insights, Inc. (2021)
2. Bender, M.A., et al.: An introduction to Bϵ-trees and write-optimization. Usenix Mag. **40**(5), 22–28 (2015). https://www.usenix.org/publications/login/oct15/bender
3. Bloom, B.H.: Space/time trade-offs in hash coding with allowable errors. Commun. ACM **13**(7), 422–426 (1970)

4. Fazackerley, S., Ould-Khessal, N., Lawrence, R.: Efficient flash indexing for time series data on memory-constrained embedded sensor devices. In: Proceedings of the 10th International Conference on Sensor Networks, SENSORNETS 2021, pp. 92–99. SCITEPRESS (2021). https://doi.org/10.5220/0010318800920099

5. Feltham, A., Ould-Khessal, N., MacBeth, S., Fazackerley, S., Lawrence, R.: Linear hashing implementations for flash memory. In: Filipe, J., Śmiałek, M., Brodsky, A., Hammoudi, S. (eds.) ICEIS 2019. LNBIP, vol. 378, pp. 386–405. Springer, Cham (2020). https://doi.org/10.1007/978-3-030-40783-4_18

6. Ferragina, P., Vinciguerra, G.: The PGM-index: a fully-dynamic compressed learned index with provable worst-case bounds. Proc. VLDB Endow. **13**(8), 1162–1175 (2020). https://doi.org/10.14778/3389133.3389135

7. Fevgas, A., Akritidis, L., Bozanis, P., Manolopoulos, Y.: Indexing in flash storage devices: a survey on challenges, current approaches, and future trends. VLDB J. **29**(1), 273–311 (2019). https://doi.org/10.1007/s00778-019-00559-8

8. Hardock, S., Koch, A., Vinçon, T., Petrov, I.: IPA-IDX: in-place appends for B-tree indices. In: 15th International Workshop on Data Management, pp. 18:1–18:3. ACM (2019). https://doi.org/10.1145/3329785.3329929

9. Kim, B., Lee, D.: LSB-tree: a log-structured B-Tree index structure for NAND flash SSDs. Des. Autom. Embed. Syst. **19**(1-2), 77–100 (2015). https://doi.org/10.1007/s10617-014-9139-4

10. Marcus, R., et al.: Benchmarking learned indexes. Proc. VLDB Endow. **14**(1), 1–13 (2020). https://doi.org/10.14778/3421424.3421425

11. Mathur, G., Desnoyers, P., Chukiu, P., Ganesan, D., Shenoy, P.: Ultra-low power data storage for sensor networks. ACM Trans. Sens. Netw. **5**(4), 1–34 (2009)

12. Na, G., Lee, S., Moon, B.: Dynamic in-page logging for B-tree index. IEEE Trans. Knowl. Data Eng. **24**(7), 1231–1243 (2012). https://doi.org/10.1109/TKDE.2011.32

13. O'Neil, P.E., Cheng, E., Gawlick, D., O'Neil, E.J.: The log-structured merge-tree (LSM-tree). Acta Informatica **33**(4), 351–385 (1996). https://doi.org/10.1007/s002360050048

14. Ould-Khessal, N., Fazackerley, S., Lawrence, R.: B-tree implementation for memory-constrained embedded systems. In: 19th International Conference on Embedded Systems, Cyber-Physical Systems, and Applications (ESCS). CSREA Press (2021)

15. Roh, H., Kim, S., Lee, D., Park, S.: AS B-tree: a study of an efficient B+-tree for SSDs. J. Inf. Sci. Eng. **30**(1), 85–106 (2014)

16. Sezer, O.B., Dogdu, E., Ozbayoglu, A.M.: Context-aware computing, learning, and big data in internet of things: a survey. IEEE Internet Things J. **5**(1), 1–27 (2018). https://doi.org/10.1109/JIOT.2017.2773600

17. Sinha, R.R., Winslett, M., Wu, K., Stockinger, K., Shoshani, A.: Adaptive bitmap indexes for space-constrained systems. In: 2008 IEEE 24th International Conference on Data Engineering, pp. 1418–1420. IEEE (2008). https://doi.org/10.1109/ICDE.2008.4497575

18. Tsiftes, N., Dunkels, A.: A database in every sensor. In: Proceedings of the 9th ACM Conference on Embedded Networked Sensor Systems, SenSys 2011, pp. 316–332. ACM (2011). https://doi.org/10.1145/2070942.2070974

19. Wu, C., Kuo, T., Chang, L.: An efficient B-tree layer implementation for flash-memory storage systems. ACM Trans. Embed. Comput. Syst. **6**(3), 19 (2007). https://doi.org/10.1145/1275986.1275991

20. Wu, K., Otoo, E.J., Shoshani, A.: Optimizing bitmap indices with efficient compression. ACM Trans. Database Syst. **31**(1), 1–38 (2006). https://doi.org/10.1145/1132863.1132864
21. Wu, K., Shoshani, A., Stockinger, K.: Analyses of multi-level and multi-component compressed bitmap indexes. ACM Trans. Database Syst. **35**(1), 1–52 (2008). https://doi.org/10.1145/1670243.1670245
22. Yin, S., Pucheral, P.: PBFilter: a flash-based indexing scheme for embedded systems. Inf. Syst. **37**(7), 634–653 (2012). https://doi.org/10.1016/j.is.2012.02.002
23. Zeinalipour-Yazti, D., Lin, S., Kalogeraki, V., Gunopulos, D., Najjar, W.: Micro-Hash: an efficient index structure for flash-based sensor devices. In: Proceedings of the FAST 2005 Conference on File and Storage Technologies, pp. 31–43. USENIX Association (2005)
24. Zhang, H., et al.: Succinct range filters. ACM Trans. Database Syst. **45**(2), 5:1–5:31 (2020). https://doi.org/10.1145/3375660

Author Index

Printed in the United States
by Baker & Taylor Publisher Services